Gillie's World

Gillie's World

Gillian McDonald Howie

ISBN: 978-976-8244-32-1

Design & Layout by Paria Publishing Co. Ltd.

Printing by Lightningsource.com

Gillie's World

Gillian McDonald Howie

ISBN: 978-976-8244-32-1

Design & Layout by Paria Publishing Co. Ltd.

Printing by Lightningsource.com

Contents

To my beloved husband Douglas John MacDonald Howie
and to our two children Catherine and Skene.

54 YEARS OF LOVING

For My Husband

For 54 years my husband taught me
That it is in giving love
That love will be returned
As slowly it dawned on me
How very much I'd come to love him
And how much a part of me he is.

Our Creator took my Love
Though he tried his best to stay
I tried my best to keep him too
But could not find a way.

I cannot find you now my Love
Though love continues just as strong
......but from a broken heart,
And how is it possible a broken heart can heal?
Because half of it is missing in your absence all too real.

And yet I must continue
To breathe and live on earth
Until one day God calls me back
To you my beloved Douglas John MacDonald Howie
When I have my second birth.

Introduction

by Ian McDonald

I have a younger brother, Archie, and four younger sisters—
Heather, Gillian, Robin and Monica. They are differently vivid
people. I think of them always as young, my little sisters. When I
was a boy they were a good part of my life. We got on well, they were
fun, my friends liked them. I recall no stresses or strains, no blurs
or buts. All my life everyone I know who knows them has said what
lovely people they are. I am a fortunate brother.

Since I left Trinidad for Cambridge at eighteen we have journeyed
far—and now Archie is in Devon, Heather in Dumfries, Gillian in
Antigua, Robin in Montreal, Monica in Bournemouth—and I have
lived my life in Guyana far away. We have not met together much
except at family reunions. Lately we have hardly met. But when
we have met it is as if they never went away in my life. There they
are—wonderful people who have lived such good lives. I love them
very much.

Gillie, no other name I ever used, filled our lives with her special
gifts of imagination and love and compassion for those who need
care and concern and saving from the ills of the world. I remember
sharp bursts of outrage, reminding me of our beloved mother—not
so much directed at anyone in particular but more a quick anger
at injustice, unfairness, cruelty, "taking advantage," the doing to
others what her heart cries out should never be done. She had the
softest of spots for helplessness.

Well, at times she might have taken things a little far. I have
not forgotten the day our dear father, expecting to surprise and
delight his wife and family, drove a brand new car up our driveway

to replace the old rattle-trap Morris which we had had for such a very long time. Expecting joy and excitement, he received it—except from Gillie who wanted to know with tears in her eyes what had happened to poor old P8152, what had been cruelly done, old P8152 who had so loyally served us for so long, how could he be just pitched away! At the very least the old car must be brought back for a ceremony of thanks and farewell. I can't remember if that happened but it was a few days before our slightly bemused father got back into Gillie's usual loving favour. Ah, Gillie, so many good memories of your fair mind and loving heart!

We have lived far apart but over the years I regularly received letters and cards from Gillie with snapshots in words of her life as she and her beloved husband Doug went from place to place in England and the West Indies wherever his job managing hotels took him, settling finally in Antigua at the beautiful family home Cliff House on wind-swept, blue oceaned Hodges Bay. I treasure these letters and cards full of *Gillieisms* and her special perceptions of the world and the people in it and the experiences we all have but Gillie especially if you see what I mean.

Some of these communications were contained in envelopes entirely covered—except for where the address was and the place for stamps—with beautifully conceived, colourful illustrations of places in Gillie's life. Perfectly etched depictions of scenes in vivid colour. I am always grateful to the gray and boring postal service that these marvelous creations get safely to me. Often Gillie appends a little note begging the postman to take good care of her letters and I like to think of him doing so with great pleasure.

And now and then Gillie would send a "story," an extended memory of hers. I recognised them as special when I got them. No one else could have written them for sure. They were water-marked Gillie. I was very pleased whenever she found the inspiration to expand a memory, add details, make it more complete. In the case of a wonderfully eccentric school headmistress Gillie came to know in Antigua, the story became a series and ended up in a deliciously amusing and delightful book called *Mrs. Wimbourne's School*. In another case I was editor of the Guyanese and West India magazine *Kyk-Over-Al* when Gillie produced her story Annie which I loved and included in an issue of the magazine. I was pleased it was specially noticed by reviewers.

So these stories have accumulated over the years and have given me and other family members much pleasure. They deserve to be published and given the chance of another life. In one or two instances I heard Gillie tell the story. She had a tentative but serious way of telling what she remembered which was absolutely Gillie, and added beautifully to the telling. I remember when she told me the story which appears here as 'Porky and the Princess,' how I laughed more and more as she grew more and more serious, on purpose, in the telling. I wish she had recorded all these stories in her own voice and way.

As it is on the page they are marvelously alive. For me, her brother who loves these stories, they will always be "Gillie's World" where our human nature is seen with singular compassion and the light of a special understanding and love shines on all the players.

IAN McDONALD

Preface

I have been writing memories of events in my life since I was a teenager and all these 'stories' are to be found jotted down in bits and pieces of my diaries throughout the years.

The stories, based on very young childhood memories, though not written out in any diary, are events that still stand out clearly in my mind. They formed a deep impression on me when they occurred.

The only stories I've had published are 'The Lost Millions' in *Treasure House—A Caribbean Anthology* published by Macmillan Caribbean, and 'Annie' which was published in *Kyk-Over-Al*. Other than these, the stories I've written were for my own need to set these different events free from my untidy, old diaries and give them a place of their very own which I felt they deserved.

I must thank my brother Ian McDonald, a well-known and loved West Indian author and poet, and my sister Robin McDonald for putting my stories into the hands of a Publisher through which they will emerge into lives of their own. There are probably many more stories in the diaries now in an old wooden cupboard in Cliff House, Antigua, which will never see the light of day as nobody has the time or energy to go through old diaries!

I am deeply grateful to my beloved husband of fifty-four years, Douglas John MacDonald Howie, for his constant love and encouragement throughout our lives together. He taught me the true meaning of love. He is deeply missed but is a part of me forever and I have dedicated this book to him and to the daughter and son he gave me and who are so much a part of us.

GILLIAN McDONALD HOWIE

Photo by Skene Howie

Cliff House

I do not know of Heaven
But, to me
My life on earth,
Now,
Is Heaven.
My husband Doug
is whistling
As he rakes the garden
and builds a wall of stone
around our hibiscus
and night jasmine;
I have just finished
my last drop
of breakfast coffee
after a swim
and a walk
with our three dogs
on Jabberwock beach.

I sit in Cliff House
Built by my grandparents
On a rocky point overlooking the sea;
The ever changing sea.
A pelican flies past,
And then five laughing gulls
Calling loudly to each other
And in the garden
The doves are crooning
In the Scarlet Cordia tree.
Dear God I wish
this could be mine forever,
But thank You
For today.

April 11, 2004

Mum's Memories

Arima, St. Joseph, Tobago

When Mum was a child in Arima she was taught mathematics at the convent by Mother Dominic. She could not understand math and Mother Dominic gave them page after page without any explanations, so Mum copied all her answers from Malia Gonsalves who sat next to her and was very good at math. Mum wondered how it was possible for anyone to look as much like a frog as Mother Dominic did.

I remember Malia Gonsalves under her married name Malia Nordman. She played the piano at weddings, anniversaries and parties. She was a lovely person. Mum tells me that Malia met and fell in love with Nordman, an American and they got married and had two children and were very happy. One day Nordman was offered a good job on a camp in Venezuela. He was to go first as there was no accommodation for wives on the camp and then he would send for Malia and the children once he was settled and found a place for his family to live. At first he wrote regularly but after three or four months the letters became fewer and then suddenly they stopped. Malia was frantic; she sent telegrams; she wrote to the Camp and received no answer. Eventually she went to Venezuela with one of her brothers and they were told that her husband had left the camp sometime before, that he had left no forwarding address and they had no idea where he was. They were told that a Venezuelan woman had moved in with him some weeks before he'd left camp, a woman who came from a family of witchcraft and love spells! Malia never did hear anything from her husband ever again—she never re-married and brought up her children with the help of her

1

brothers and her lovely piano playing which she did completely by ear, she'd never had a lesson in her life.

Then Mum's family moved to St. Joseph and Mum attended St. Joseph's Convent and was taught math by Mother Patrick and learned nothing at all. Mother Patrick was old and had a red face and she would say to her class, "Now what was the last page we did?" and the class would say. "Number seven Mother," and Mother Patrick would say, "alright, now we will do number eight" and for several days they would do number eight and planned the games of skip and jacks they would play at Break.

Then Mum's family moved to Tobago for a while. Mum remembers the Washerwoman in Tobago well. She would come twice a week with a big wooden tray on her head to collect all the dirty washing and bring back all the clean, ironed clothes. What a job it must have been to carry that tray full of clothes on your head from the village to the house and back.....and ironing in those days without electricity—putting the heavy irons onto hot coals, you had to know exactly when to take the iron off.....and washing in big tubs with wooden scrubbing boards and coarse soap. Sometimes the washerwoman would bring her daughter, who was Mum's age, with her, and Mum looked forward to the days when 'Black Doll' came and Mum and Black Doll played 'Hands, Knees and Bumpsa Daisy' and 'Clap Hands.' Mum always knew her as 'Black Doll' and never did hear what her name really was. Mum would run out to meet Washerwoman and Black Doll whenever she saw them coming.

One day Mum's Nanny, Frances, told Mum that her Godchild had died the night before of peritonitis caused by a burst appendix and this afternoon instead of walking in the Savannah they would go by her godchild's home to pay last respects, but Mum was not to tell Grandma.

They went and there was Frances's godchild lying on her bed dressed in her white First Communion Dress with her First Communion Veil on her head and white roses in her hands. Mum said she looked quite lovely and not at all frightening. She never did repeat this incident.

Mum's First Baby

I was chatting with Mum at lunch today, 22nd April 1986, and she was telling me about Ian's birth. That was 53 years ago. Mum and Dad lived in a house at the top of Carmody Road, St. Augustine, and in those days women usually had their babies at home. Old Dr. Gibbon delivered Ian. He was a big baby, nearly 10 pounds, and Mum had to have stitches after the birth. Dr. Gibbon told Mum he'd stitch right away and she had eight stitches. Then Dr. Gibbon tied each of Mum's legs to a bedpost explaining that the stitches would heal better if she could not move around. After lying flat on her back for a couple of hours Mum began to feel very uncomfortable. She complained to Nurse Dottin that she would not be able to sleep like this and the nurse told her that as soon as Dr. Gibbon went home she would untie Mum's legs but she was to be very careful how she turned in bed. Mum said, "What a relief that was!"

Mum said it was so hard to enjoy her first baby. Nurse Dottin told her that he had to be breast fed every three hours on the dot and the three hours must be counted from the exact time she'd *finished* feeding him until the time she started again. Then the worry was if the baby was getting enough milk. Nurse Dottin said the only way to know this was to weigh the baby after each feed. Sometimes he'd put on one ounce, but there was panic if he'd only put on quarter of an ounce.

The next thing was Mum had been given a lot of baby books telling her exactly how a baby must be brought up from birth to its best advantage. Mum wanted only the best for her baby so she was determined to follow the books exactly. One of the big rules was that you must not pick up your baby too often, certainly not

Dad and Ian in 1935

every time he cried; usually only to feed and change him and for other certain reasons. Mum said she used to stand by the door looking at her baby waving his arms and legs in the air and screaming his head off and she'd start to cry as well as she was desperately longing to hold him in her arms and cuddle him—but no—the book said this would make the baby too dependent on its mother in later years. Once the baby was fed and changed he should be put back into bed; you must cut out the silly cuddling and fussing. Grandma Emmy Seheult (Mum's Mum) told Mum off about this and said it was all nonsense; she had always picked up her babies when they cried; but Mum argued that Gran was being old fashioned and the modern way must be better as it would help the baby grow into an independent, self adjusted individual.

Mum said this lasted for about three weeks by which time she was completely frustrated and depressed and suddenly she couldn't stand it anymore, started picking up her baby and cuddling him, sitting in the rocking chair singing lullabies and saying little coo-coo things to him as he held her finger tightly in his hand and coo-cooed back. The books went into the wastepaper basket and Mum and baby were very happy from then on.

Mum had five more children and went on her own intuition for all the rest of us. We've all grown into well-adjusted human beings.

I remember Mum when she was in a warm, loving mood holding her arms wide open and saying to whichever of us was there, "I love you all *Big So*" and giving us hugs and kisses.

Trips to England when Mum and Dad were in their 20s

Mum and Dad would have been in their 20s. They would travel in the Lady Boats. It cost fifty pounds return for a double cabin and the trip took two weeks. A nice cabin, good meals, pleasant company, an average of about 60 passengers, lots of deck space with long chairs, deck tennis, bridge and card games in the evenings and a stop at every port. The Lady Boats would start from Guyana (then British Guiana) and stop at most islands on the way.....Trinidad, Barbados, St. Lucia, Antigua, St. Kitts, and at least three others.

On arrival in London, Mum and Dad stayed at the Balmoral Hotel very near to the centre of London, opposite to Whiteleys. They paid two pounds fifty pence a week for a double room, breakfast and dinner. Early morning tea and biscuits was served in the room free of charge. If you wanted lunch you would tell the desk at breakfast-time and a three course lunch would be served for one shilling extra.

Mum and Dad did not have to save for these holidays as they could cover everything with Dad's monthly salary, which in these times would seem poverty stricken.

In these days of advanced technology there are no more boats to travel in. People rush from point A to B in jet airliners, squished into small seats for hours at a time, paying thousands each trip and having to save for years for any holiday abroad. Life is a constant rush and if you can afford a holiday, it is usually a very short one, as the money to cover hotels, guest houses, food, and entertainment very soon runs out.

Mum in U.K. 1935

In Mum and Dad's young days, Dad would get two weeks holiday a year and three months holiday every three years.

The lady who ran The Balmoral Hotel was Dalmer Dew's sister Olive. Olive eventually left The Balmoral and went to work as housekeeper for a very rich Englishman. When he died he left Olive everything he had. Olive, who had no immediate family, died six months later and no one knows what became of the money.

Poems Mum taught us when we were children:

Ma Gros Dent

Ma Gros Dent was a witch indeed
And a grand old witch was she
She sold her soul to the devil twice
And cheated him of his fee;
But when it came to the third contract
The devil he swore an oath
That he would have Ma Gros Dent's soul
Though she was ever so loath.

"If I must go then go I must" she cried, "alack, alay,
So make your back both strong and broad
And fly with me with heed
For I'm old and frail and if I fall
Oh! It will be the devil indeed."

The devil he flew over Montserrat
With Ma Gros Dent on his back
But when he saw Tucuche's height
He cried, "Ochone Alack!
I can never fly so high," said he,
"With such an awful load!"
So he turned from the hills
And made for The Isles
And he spilt her on the road.

At Diego Martin it's known for certain
She came down with a thud,
For witches, there, enough and to spare
Have sprung from the witch's blood.

Her heart is buried at Hart's Cut
Her head in Gasparee
And there in sooth
You may find her tooth
A good mile out to sea.
The cave is Ma Gros Dent's brain pan
The other cave's her eye,
And if you don't believe it now,
Why neither in truth do I!

By Judge Russell (who wrote *Legends of The Bocas*). Mum knew
Judge Russell and his wife Stella well.

***

Mum learned this at Miss Clark's School in Tobago - aged 7.

George Ninevah
In California mountains
A hunter bold was he,
Keen his eye and sure his aim
As any you may see.

A little Indian boy
Followed him everywhere
Eager to share the hunter's joy
The hunter's meal to share.

One day, as in a cleft,
Between two mountains steep
Shut in both right and left
That questing way they keep.

They suddenly see two grizzly bears
With hunger fierce and fell
Rush at them unawares
Along the narrow dell.

The boy turned around with screams
And ran with terror wild
One of the pair of savage beasts
Pursued the shrieking child.

The hunter raised his gun
He knew one chance was all
And through the boys pursuing foe
He sent his only ball.

The other on George Ninevah
Came on with dreadful force
The hunter held his empty gun
And prayed for some resource.

The hunter turned and stood unarmed
He met him face to face
And there at the edge of the lonely wood
He knew he'd lost the race.

The bear he came to a full stop
in front of Ninevah
Who like a marble statue stood
His useless rifle in his hands
But a piece of harmless wood.

They looked each other in the eye
The hunter and the bear
Then the bear he slowly turned
and walked away
Towards his home, the wood.

What thoughts were in that huge bear's mind
It would be hard to say;
What thoughts were in George Ninevah's
I'd rather guess than say!

***

This poem was composed on a picnic Down the Islands to the Island named Caledonia and sung to the tune of "Oh my Darling Clementine"

To an Isla called Caledonia
Not so very far away
With Aunty Norah (Great Grandma)
And plenty more - a
And her daughter Dolly Gray (Aunty Muriel).

And then there was Bro (Great Grandma's brother)
And then there's Audrey (Aunty Violet's sister)
And Copybook the Master Man (Professor Low, Headmaster of Queen's Royal College)
Skipper Burly nicknamed Curly (in love with Aunt Anna)
And the Miss's Aunty Ann (Aunt Anna; she didn't marry Curly because he wasn't good enough.)

This line refers to Stella (Aunty Violet's sister)
And of them all she did the talking
Most of all at dinner time
And is it not shocking
That a blue stocking (schoolgirl)
Should be talking all the time?

Before I go I must enjoin you
To be careful what you say
For your words
When least you think it
May be taken the wrong way.

When I've gone to
Lands far distant
Sailed away across the sea
Don't forget
But sometimes think of

Yours sincerely
H.R.C.
H. R. Clayton

Porky
and the Princess

I was six years old and lived with my Mum and Dad, brother Ian aged 12, sister Heather aged 10 and baby sister Robin aged 2 in our home in Carmody Road, St. Augustine, Trinidad. The rest of our family—Monica and Archie—were yet to be born.

My best friend was Maryanne Shepherd, also six years old, who lived 'just down the road' on Circular Road, a road which surrounded The Imperial College of Tropical Agriculture (I.C.T.A.). My Dad had studied tropical agriculture there and then for a few years after he graduated, had been a professor there, but now he worked with Gordon Grant & Company Limited, as Supervisor for their estates, mostly coffee and cocoa but there were some coconut estates as well.

One day Maryanne ran over to our home in Carmody road in great excitement to tell me that Princess Alice a *real* princess from England, was coming next week to plant a tree in front of the main building of I.C.T.A. and that her parents were invited and were going to take her with them. She asked if my Mum and Dad had been invited. I said I didn't know and I ran inside to find Mum and ask her. When I found Mum she told me they hadn't been invited and maybe it was only the staff and their wives—Maryanne's Dad was a professor at I.C.T.A. I felt devastated—a REAL princess would be coming next week, and be so close to us, but I could not go and see her. I knew so much about princesses from my story books, all so beautiful in sparkling dresses and tiaras in their hair, some even had magic wands. It seemed to me that Maryanne must be the luckiest girl in the whole world.

The next day Maryanne came over to tell me that her Mum said I could come with them to see Princess Alice plant the tree. What excitement! I ran to tell Mum and Dad and they said I must go over and thank Mr. and Mrs. Shepherd. I ran over to Maryanne's house accompanied by my little dog Porky. I loved Porky very much and he followed me everywhere. He had been given to me as a present from Maryanne about a year ago when the Shepherd's dog Wendy had puppies and Maryanne told me that her Mum and Dad were not able to sell the puppies because Wendy had made friends with a common dog and Wendy was a pedigree. I didn't understand what this meant and neither did Maryanne, but I was thrilled with my gift. My Mum and Dad were not so thrilled and told me I would have to look after him and house train him or I would not be allowed to keep him. As Porky grew up he did not look at all like Wendy..... Wendy was small and white with short legs and curly hair, Porky was about twice her size with straight rough hair, pointed ears and a short tail that for some curious reason wagged up and down instead of from side to side. He was a black and tan. The whole family gradually grew to love Porky and Mum and Dad approved of him because he was a great hunter and killed all the rats that used to eat our chicken's eggs. I arrived at the Shepherds' home to thank Mrs. Shepherd for inviting me and she told me I must meet them at 3 o'clock and from there we would all walk across the Savannah to the Main Building. Princess Alice was arriving at 4 o'clock. Then she told me that I mustn't bring Porky with me. She said this because she knew that Porky followed me everywhere. I promised her that I would leave Porky at home.

Now the excitement of going to see Princess Alice plant the tree began. Today was Saturday so I had four days to get ready. Mum chose my 'party' dress which was pink and white with frills and tied in a big bow at the back. On Tuesday Mum washed my hair, then put it into 'pappyots' to make curls. When my hair dried Mum untied the 'pappyots' and my whole head was covered in golden curls; then Mum put a big pink bow in amongst my curls. I put on a pair of white socks and my new shoes and I was ready. I put Porky in our bedroom (my older sister Heather, and I, shared a bedroom) and closed the door (I couldn't lock it as there was no lock on the door), reminding Mum and Dad that Porky must not come out. Mum and Dad gave me hugs and kisses and said they wanted to know all about it when I came back. Then I set out for Maryanne's home running, hopping and skipping down Carmody road (six year old children *never* walk sedately) where the asphalt

Princess Alice planted the palm tree on the right. A few
weeks afterwards the other one was planted.

felt warm and soft under my feet. Carmody road was made of pure
asphalt and it was very black. At lunchtime in the heat of the sun
it felt soft under one's feet and at night it was as hard as rock. This
ashpalt came from Trinidad's famous Pitch Lake.

When I arrived at the Shepherd's home everyone was almost
ready. Maryanne also had on her best dress and new shoes, Mrs.
Shepherd had on a lovely straw hat with a flower in it and Professor
Shepherd was dressed in a suit. We all walked across the Savannah
over to the Main Building and met with a group of Professors,
their wives and children who were standing on the lawn in front
of the Main Building. The ladies all wore hats and the men were
all dressed in suits. Everyone was chatting. The Principal of the
College was at the front of the group with his wife; everyone waiting
for Princess Alice to arrive.

Suddenly someone said, 'That's her car' and there was a hushed
silence. My heart was beating with excitement. A big shining black
car drove slowly over to where we all stood and the Principal and
his wife walked towards it. When the car stopped, the chauffeur,
in full uniform, opened the front door and quickly went to open
the back door for Princess Alice and by this time the Principal was
there to take Princess Alice's hand as she stepped out of the car; but
could this really be Princess Alice?! My heart sank. Could this stout
old lady dressed in a grey suit, small grey hat and black shoes, really
be a Princess?? I looked towards the car hoping and praying that
even now the *real* Princess would appear; but no; now the Principal

and his wife were shaking hands with this very ordinary lady and welcoming her to The Imperial College Of Tropical Agriculture.

It was still taking me time to accept that this was really Princess Alice. Now the Principal was making a speech but none of it sank in. Maryanne nudged my arm to tell me, "you're not clapping" and as I started to put my hands together in a half-hearted way I noticed a group of dogs further over on the Savannah barking and playing and surely *not*, but surely *yes*, there was Porky in the midst of them. I prayed that Porky would not come over as I tried to edge myself behind the tall man beside me. The Principal's speech was now over and he, his wife and Princess Alice made their way over to the well prepared place where the tree was already planted. A big hole had been dug, the Royal Palm was already inside the hole and re-covered with soil. All Princess Alice had to do was empty a small spadeful of earth onto the tree. A shining little spade had been 'specially bought' for the occasion and already had a small amount of earth in it. The Principal handed the spade to Princess Alice.... while all this was happening I saw Porky leaving the pack of dogs and start sniffing the air and at the same time heading towards us. A feeling of dread and impending doom now filled my already sad and disappointed little six year old heart. I felt like screaming and edged myself further behind the tall man next to me.....then just as Princess Alice was about to empty her spadeful of earth Porky came up to her, sniffed the tree, and before anyone could stop him he lifted his leg against the tree. The Principal shouted at him and shooed him away while many in the audience made sounds of disapproval. I felt as if I was going to die. Maryanne said to me, "That was Porky" and I managed to say, "That was *not*," but as soon as the event was over and the Principal and his wife left the grounds with Princess Alice, I turned and ran home as fast as my legs could go. Porky met me halfway across the Savannah and ran home with me. When I got home I ran up the stairs into my bedroom, jumped into bed, pulled the sheet over my head and cried bitterly.

Mum had noticed me running up the stairs and came to ask me what had happened and I was crying so much that at first I couldn't say anything; but Mum put her arms around me and I gradually calmed down enough to tell her that Porky had arrived at The Planting of The Tree Ceremony and he'd lifted his leg against the tree. Mum said nothing; when I looked up at her she had her hand over her face and there seemed to be tears in her eyes and

I knew she was probably too shocked to speak. I said, "I know it was a terrible thing Mum but please, please don't let them come for me" and I started sobbing again. Mum held me tight and said that she and Dad would *never* let anyone take me away; but then I reminded Mum that they were almost sure to come for Porky and Mum said they would keep Porky safe as well.

The days passed and nothing terrible happened to either myself or Porky.

Looking back it was after this 'terrible' event, starting with my fairytale princess stepping out of the car, that a page in my life turned, my fairytale books were read less often and in their place my interest graduated to books like Heidi, Shadow the Sheepdog, Black Beauty.....

Porky I loved and treasured all his life and my love for animals never changed.

Maracas River 1930s

The Lost Millions

I was about eight years old at the time and had been out with friends to a river in Maracas Valley where we spent the morning swimming and playing in the rock pools. Oh those rivers in Trinidad; how beautiful they are! There we all were jumping over rocks and in-between rocks, splashing each other and diving from the smooth, firm rocks into the crystal clear pool where the drops of water looked like diamonds in the sun when we threw our arms in the air. Those beautiful rivers surrounded by bamboo trees, and Immortelles, those tall majestic trees with their bright orange flowers and the equally tall and beautiful yellow poui with wild cocoa lilies growing underneath and the birds and the butterflies of different shapes and sizes flying in and out.

In a smaller pool near the edge of the river swam hundreds of fish called millionfish or 'millions' darting in-between rocks and into the deeper pool below as the water flowed in and out. Millions are a lovely tiny fish about as big as an adults thumbnail. They are shining silver in colour with a small red stripe in-between the silver scales and I seem to remember a blue stripe as well—a turquoise blue.

I lay on a flat rock and watched them for a while, fascinated. Then I decided to catch some and take them home with me. I caught about ten and put them into a small plastic bag with water in it, already planning where I would put them when I got home—I would put them into the big plastic basin Mum had under the wash-basin. I would feed them on biscuit crumbs and as well as filling the basin with water I would put some rocks in it so they could swim in and out of the rocks and they would be so happy. My friend Maryanne also caught some millions and put them into a plastic bag with the same idea in mind.

When I arrived home it was nearly lunch time. The cook and Mum were preparing lunch—Mum always made our delicious desserts herself —and Dad was having a bridge party with his male friends in the drawing-room from where we could hear talking and laughter. I was longing to show everyone my beautiful millions but first I must look for a bowl to put them into so their lovely colours would glint as they swam around and everyone would see and exclaim at their beauty.

I poured them out of my plastic bag into a jug I found on the shelf, filled the jug with more water to keep my fish happy and then put the jug on top of the refrigerator for safekeeping while I went to look for a bowl to put them into. I wanted a glass bowl but the nearest thing I could find was one of Mum's pyrex dessert bowls. I rushed back with my pyrex bowl to find that the jug had disappeared. The top of the 'fridge was bare, empty! I asked Mum if she'd seen my jug on top of the 'fridge. "*Your* jug child? Your Dad just put some ice into it and took it into the drawing-room to mix drinks."

I ran into the drawing-room in a panic, into the middle of the men's Bridge party (there were three tables of fours) where I was usually not allowed, rushing up to Dad, "Dad, Dad, have you got my jug of millions?" and as I said this I saw my jug on the small side-table with a bottle of whisky beside it and a silver ice-pail and ice holder. With relief I picked it up, and — it was empty!

"Dad!" I screamed, staring into the jug, "where are my millions?" My Dad looked over his hand of cards with a puzzled expression and said affectionately, "Your millions Gillie?" "Yes Dad, my millions; they were in this jug," and I held up the empty jug; "I caught them in Maracas River this morning. They're beautiful...." "*your millions were in this jug?*" said Dad, less affectionately and paying more attention to me now.

With a look of horrified amusement on his face Dad turned to his partners "Well friends! We've just drunk Gillies millions!" and he showed them the empty jug. Everyone picked up their glasses and stared into them. Dad's, Uncle Frank's, Uncle Gordon's glasses were all empty but Uncle Cory had some left in his, and as he peered into his glass he said, with a roar of laughter, "Well boys, there's one in here!" and he held up his half filled glass.

I ran over to Uncle Cory with the jug in my hand to rescue my one million only to have him look over his glasses at me with a kind and sympathetic smile, "I'm sorry my dear, but this thing is as dead as a doornail!"

There was a pause and then Uncle Cory put the glass up to his mouth with a flourish and drank everything—"Might as well put it to rest," he laughed. I left the drawing-room where men's laughter and 'joie de vivre' filled the air. The men from the other tables had come over to see what was happening and were joining in the laughter.

As I left the room my feeling of horrified amazement at what had happened to my millions was reduced to a feeling of relief at the way Dad and his friends had taken to the thought of swallowing them. As I realised what was happening, a feeling of worry that they would be very upset with me dawned on me and my overall relief at the way the whole thing had gone, overcame the sorrow at my millions fate!

When I saw my friend Maryanne the following day she told me that all her millions had perished! She'd put them into a bowl her father had used for disinfectant without washing it out first and this morning all the poor things were floating on top of the water!

I told her what had happened to mine with a sorrowful air but as I reached the end of my story and the fate of my fish I started to giggle and then to laugh so that it was difficult to finish as I tried to tell Maryanne about the scene in the drawing-room and Uncle Cory and .....

We sat there with tears streaming down our cheeks—but I'm afraid they were tears of laughter.

In the years that followed I often swam in the Maracas river but I never again caught anything. Instead I'd sit on a rock and watch 'my' millions as they swam happily in their own home and knew that they were where they should be and not in 'prison' in someone's plastic bowl—or worse!

1 Carmody Road House 1943

Memories of Carmody Road

St. Augustine, Trinidad 1944/45

I grew up loving animals. From the time I was a very little girl I wanted a pet of my own. I lived in a happy home surrounded by three siblings (two more were yet to come) and a devoted Mum and Dad. There was an acre of land and on the bottom half, Mum and Dad kept chickens and ducks. There was a huge saman tree in the corner, a sweetlime hedge along the driveway near to the kitchen entrance and our chickens and ducks running free. Mum and Dad kept these so that we'd have our own eggs, but we children never guessed that the delicious roast chicken we had for lunch every Sunday also came from 'our' brood. I often chased the chickens to try and cuddle them and assure them how much I loved them but they'd run off in different directions and if I did catch one of them it squawked and looked nervous and ran away in relief when I let it go; so instead of chasing them I'd feed them their corn kernels, throwing handfuls for them and then they'd all come running. Dad brought home bags of whole corn kernels from the estates and we'd grind them in the little machine to the size we wanted. Ram, our gardener, usually ground the corn and sometimes I would do it when I wanted corn of my own for the chickens. Our chickens also had fun having their dust baths on a dry day digging a hole under the hedge and throwing the dust all over themselves.....strangely they would look very clean when they finally shook themselves.

I also often helped our cook Alice look for eggs—under the sweetlime hedge, under the saaman tree in amongst the anthuriums—lovely brown eggs.....Dad always said he preferred brown eggs.

.

We also had a cow. Dad brought home a cow and her little calf from the estates so that we would have our own milk. Ram, who had a cow of his own, milked the cow every morning, the milk spurting into a shining metal bucket in a steady stream and then we'd boil it before bottling it and putting it into the fridge. One day I asked Ram to show me how to milk the cow and sat beside him on my haunches—the way Ram sat when he was milking—and he showed me that I must bend my thumb against the nipple, put my other fingers around it and squeeze as hard as I could; but no matter how hard I squeezed only a few drops and sometimes if I was lucky, a trickle, would go into the bucket. Much to Ram's relief I soon gave it up; but I always loved to watch him milking the cow, sitting on his haunches and shouting from time to time, "Coaww! Coaww!" when she flung her tail back and forth to keep away the flies and sometimes her tail would brush across Ram's head as it swung. I loved to take the full bucket of snow-white milk back to the kitchen where Alice would put it on to boil and wash out the bucket with boiling water. Dad would bring bundles of grass back from the estates for the cow and give half of it to Ram for his cow.

COCKELEY AND WHOLLY

.....Then one day a miracle happened! And I was given the first pet of my own. It happened like this.....we had a hen who was sitting on five eggs when suddenly, halfway through the setting period she lost all interest in what she was doing and refused to go back to her nest; but luckily at the same time there was a duck who was also sitting on her own eggs so Mum quickly took the five eggs and put them under the duck. Well—ducks take longer to hatch than chickens and one morning we woke up to find five tiny, fluffy, beautiful little chickens chirping their heads off, calling for their mummy. When the chickens hatched the duck was horrified and pushed them all out of her nest wanting absolutely nothing to do with them.

To my great joy Mum gave them to me to take care of and from then on they became the centre of my life. The first thing I did was to grind some corn into very small pieces for them to eat and along with the corn I crumbled bread into tiny pieces as well. I would sit with them for hours watching them out of the corner of my eye as I played Jacks on the concrete pavement around the house. They stayed very close to me at first and every now and then I'd give them a handful of corn and breadcrumbs. At night I put them into a cardboard box and locked them in the storeroom where they were safe from predators.

'My' chickens followed me everywhere and as I was not allowed to bring them into the house I now spent most of my time in the garden with them, feeding them and playing with them. I would sit on the ground and they'd gather around me and I'd fold them into my skirt. When I wanted to stand up I'd empty them back out onto the ground and give them a handful of food. One day when it was pouring with rain I put them all into their cardboard box and took them up to my bedroom.

As they grew up we could see that there were two Roosters and three Hens. My three hens went off with the other chickens in the garden as they matured although they always were tamer than any of the other hens; but the two roosters, Cockeley and Wholly, stayed very close to me. They were both beautiful. Cockeley was very handsome with shining red and gold feathers all over, a wonderful curved tail and a red crown. He had a loud crow 'cock-a-doodle-doo' that was louder than any other cockerel in our brood. We'd hear him early in the morning as he slept in an orange tree close to our bedroom window—he'd start crowing before the sun came up.....I'd hear him and then go back to sleep. Wholly was also very handsome but had completely different coloured feathers, all his feathers were white and black and he also had a beautiful curved tail and a red crown on his head like Cockeley. They were the two best-looking Roosters I'd ever seen, maybe Cockeley *the* best-looking of them all...but eventually Wholly, like the hens, gradually became less tame and moved in with all the other chickens.....not so Cockeley who always stayed close to us. As soon as I came out in the morning Cockeley would be there and I often stayed outside so he could be close to me while I looked through my nursery-rhyme books or played Jacks or Marbles and Cockeley would sit beside me; sometimes he gave himself a dust bath or dug up a worm or two and then would call all the hens who would gather excitedly around him; sometimes he had fights with one or other of the cockerels (but I never remember him fighting with Wholly) and I'd hear loud noises and see a feather or two flying in the air. If I saw him fighting I'd always try and separate them and was only successful if I threw a bucket of water over them.

Gillie and Cockeley

I remember two crisis points in Cockeley's life; the first was when his feet became terribly swollen and he had difficulty walking. This came about because he wanted to be as close to me as possible at night and somehow managed to jump from branch to branch of the orange tree to one of the top branches which was near to our bedroom window. However getting down in the morning was another thing and Cockeley didn't have the patience to jump down from branch to branch so he'd just jump from the top branch onto the ground below and after a few weeks of this his feet became very swollen and they must have been very painful because he started to limp. Mum and Dad advised me to lock him in the storeroom at night until his feet got better. I did this and his feet did get better but it took two or three weeks. During the time that he was sleeping in the storeroom Dad brought home a man from his estates who cut the orange tree much shorter so when Cockeley was once more free at night and went back to the orange tree the highest branch was much lower to the ground; and once more I could hear him crowing in the morning, only now I could not see him as well.

Cockeley's 2nd crisis was nearly fatal and I only heard the story from Mum years later—Mum and Dad had the problem every Sunday of which chicken to catch for our roast chicken lunch and then showing it to Ram our gardener, who then caught it and beheaded it under the tap on the side of the house where the garage was. Mum and Dad had organized this to take place while the children were in church so we would never realize that our delicious Sunday Lunch was one of own chickens. Mum was usually with us at Church and really it was Dad who showed Ram which chicken to catch and Dad had on different occasions pointed out the children's pets to Ram and told him they must not be touched.....and now overtime the Sunday chicken was left to Ram and Alice, our cook. By the time we got home from church the chicken was ready to be put into the oven of our Esse stove. Once Ram had caught our neighbour's chicken and we had him for lunch never realizing that he belonged to Marjorie and Frank Allen. Worse still he was the pet of their children Carol and Christopher. That day he had come into our garden through a hole he'd dug in the hedge. Mum and Dad never saw him. They apologized profusely to Aunty Marge and Uncle Frank and gave them a rooster in return but of course it would not ever be the same for Carol and Christopher.

On this Sunday however things were slightly different. Dad was lying in his long chair listening to Wimbledon on his Pye radio— Dad's Pye radio was so big it took up all the space on the table next to his long chair—and he told us he could not drop us at church so we must get ready early and catch a Roving Taxi on the Eastern Main road. So we got dressed and left early, taking a short cut across the Savannah of the Imperial College of Tropical Agriculture; then all we had to do was cross the railway line at Mr. Defue's station and from there we were on the Eastern Main Road where we would wave down a Roving Taxi heading for Tunapuna. It would be ten cents each there and ten cents back. Our church was on the side of the Eastern Main Road in Tunapuna. Mum and baby Robin did not come. Before Ian, Heather and I left I heard Dad saying to Mum, "Ram has just arrived Thellie and he's as drunk as a Lord." By this time Mum and Dad had more or less left it to Ram on Sunday and they also knew that Ram knew Cockeley and Wholly very well and had been told on many different occasions not to touch them......on this day however catching one of our wilder chickens was too much for Ram in the state he was in, and seeing Cockeley walking behind him hoping for some corn, Ram bent down, picked up Cockeley, took his cutlass and headed for the garden tap. Mum heard Ram arrive and she also heard a surprised and indignant squawk which sounded familiar and ran to the back upstairs window at the top of the stairs that overlooked the back garden. She saw what was happening and *screamed* at Ram to put Cockeley down—just in time. My pet rooster lived on for many years after this, ruling all the hens, following me around when I was in the garden and sleeping in the orange tree next to my bedroom window.

It wasn't long after the episode with Ram and Cockeley that Mum and Dad found homes for all their clucking chickens and waddling ducks except for Cockeley, Wholly and about five hens who gave us lovely brown eggs for breakfast. It was a great relief to Mum not to have the Sunday chicken worry about; now she ordered our Sunday chicken from our grocer Willie Kong-Ting who had it delivered by bicycle with Mum's other groceries which were in a basket attached to the front of the bicycle; and now Mum could concentrate on starting the beautiful garden she had always wanted.

TRAVELLING BY TRAIN

I remember the train line that we had to cross from Circular Road to get onto the Eastern Main Road. Where the cars crossed there were gates and the Trainman (as we called him) Mr. Defue (Day-foo) used to close the gates when the train was passing. He had a wooden 'office' next to the line. If Mum and I wanted to take the train into Port-of-Spain, Mr. Defue would flag it down with a red flag; if there was no one waiting at his station, Mr. Defue waved the green flag.

One morning Mum called to me to get dressed because we were going into town by train. Mum needed to get a few things for me and some things for herself and the rest of the family. It was going to be a very eventful day for me. At that time I was five years old and going through my crisis of not being able to read. The thing is that I loved reading. I looked forward to the stories Mum would read to us at bedtime and I loved going through my little story books where I'd learned to read small one-syllable words and sometimes two-syllables. Mum had told me how good I was, so when I started my first school with Mrs. Hazel who lived next door to us, I was very proud of my reading and when Mrs. Hazel told me, "Now Gillian, you will really have to improve on your reading. You are slower than any of the other children," I was totally shocked. So shocked that when it was my turn to read to Mrs. Hazel, I couldn't read any of the words on the page in front of me. I shed tears when I got home and told Mum that Mrs. Hazel said I couldn't read; and when Mum opened a book in front of me, a book I'd read to Mum many times before, I couldn't read a word in it. The only thing I could remember was my ABC. After this the terrible fear of, "Will I read well?" was a question I would ask Mum and Dad every night when I went to bed. It all seemed more terrible when it was dark somehow as I lay there in my bed thinking to myself that I would turn out to be the only person in the world who could not read. Eventually Mum went to see Mrs. Hazel and asked her not to worry about my reading and not to ask me to read and assured her that she would do the lessons with me at home; and Mum did, but still the page of mixed up letters and words stared out at me and still the terrible fear of never being able to read kept me awake at night. On this day that Mum decided to go into town by train I had been going through the fear of not being able to read for some time; but now it was morning, Cockeley was crowing, the sun was shining, I was going into town with Mum in the train and all seemed well with the world. Mum and I walked across the Imperial College of Tropical Agriculture Savannah onto Circular road and Mr. Defue's Train Gates. We said, "Good morning Mr. Defue" to him and Mum told him we were going into Port-of-Spain by train. So Mr. Defue closed the gates when he knew the train to Port-of-Spain was coming and went out to the line with his red flag to wave it down. The train came chugging down the line and came to a stop with a long screech. The Conductor opened the door of a carriage and Mum and I stepped in (very exciting for a five year old), then Mum paid the Conductor for two tickets which he got from a little machine that was kept in a bag over his shoulder. He had on a uniform with brass buttons and a cap. Mum and I then walked up the passage and into an empty carriage. The carriage was very nice with a long covered sofa-bench. The sofa-bench was soft and cozy to sit on and covered in a material with all sorts of flowers on it and so was the back of the sofa-bench. In front of us was a long polished table to put things on, if you wished. There was another sofa-bench facing the table but nobody else came in. The Conductor had blown his whistle once Mum and I were in the carriage and the train started off, at first chug-chugging slowly and then into a regular chug, chug, chug which was a comforting noise as we went by scenery we never saw from the road.

The train stopped in Curepe, St.Joseph. San Juan and Laventille before coming to a final stop at the Main Station in Port-of-Spain. Mum and I walked from there to the main shopping street, Frederick Street, where Mum got all the different things she needed from all the different shops and bought a present for each one of us as well. For my big brother Ian, she bought two soldiers for his army. Ian had a large army of soldiers from all the different battalions and collected a few more whenever he could. We were in the midst of World War II and our Dad's brother, our uncle Arthur McDonald was in the R.A.F. where he was knighted for his role in the Battle of Britain and became Air Marshall Sir Arthur McDonald.

Ian also had a wonderful collection of stamps and lots of albums to put all his different stamps into. In those days we got lots of letters; the Postman came every day bringing letters from all over the world and Mum and Dad always kept the envelopes for Ian who would un-stick the stamps by holding the envelope over the steam from a boiling kettle. I often wanted to help him but he said I might tear the stamp, so I would just stand and watch.

Then Mum bought a paper doll set for Heather and told me to look for a book in the line of books that said "5 Year Olds." She bought a toy for baby Robin. I found a book with a wonderful cover of princesses with crowns, fairies with wings, heroes and ogres, a little girl, a little boy and a fluffy dog. I couldn't wait to find out what it was all about. Mum bought a Woman's Own magazine for herself. Then we walked up the stairs to the second floor of Stephen's where there was a lovely restaurant that looked over the whole shop down below. Mum ordered a cup of tea and a pastelle and I had a coconut ice cream in a cone and it was delicious. When we were finished we went downstairs and Mum called for a taxi to take us to the railway station. Once comfortably back in our carriage Mum handed me the book she'd bought for me and settled down to read her Woman's Own. I had begged Mum to read my book to me but Mum said no, she would read it tonight and I must just look at all the pictures. I looked right through my book page after page and the little boy's name was Paul, the girl's name was Mary and the little dog's name was Bazooka and all the adventures they had. I started reading it out to Mum and Mum put down her magazine and listened carefully, then she hugged me and said, "Gillie darling you've read the whole book!" I was astounded as it dawned on me 'I Can Read, I Can Read' and I shed tears of joy all over my little book.

I never looked back after that, beginning to read all my sister's old books and anything I could find that looked interesting. The days of not being able to read faded into the distance but were never forgotten.....as I remember them now and that momentous train ride with Mum where all my reading problems ended.

TRAM RIDES AROUND THE QUEEN'S PARK SAVANNAH

I remember some afternoons Dad driving us into town to 84 Dundonald Street to see Grandma Emmy Sehuelt who, after Grandpa Leo Sehuelt died, lived there with her sister Muriel Gray (whose husband had also died) and Great Aunt Anna Collins and Great Grandma Nora Collins. My big brother Ian used to board with them during the week when he started school at Queen's Royal College. When we arrived at 84 Dundonald street, Dad, Ian and Heather, all dressed in their tennis whites, went to play tennis at Tranquillity Tennis Club. Mum and I and my baby sister Robin stayed with Grandma and sometimes if it was a nice bright afternoon Mum and Gran would say, "Let's go down to the Rock Gardens" and I was thrilled because that meant we would walk up to the Queen's Park Savannah and take a tram to the Rock Gardens. I loved going around the Queen's Park Savannah in a tram. The trams were open-sided and you sat on a bench with a handle to hold onto. As the tram went around the Savannah you could see everything and Mum and Gran pointed out on one side all the big and beautiful homes as we passed, some, like Stollmeyer's Castle,

29

had turrets and towers and all of them had different but beautiful architecture and then there was Ian's school, Queen's Royal College, the green Savannah seemed to stretch forever on the other side. When the tram stopped at the Rock Gardens we all got out and Mum, Gran and two year old Robin walked down the steps into the beautiful garden itself with lily ponds and rocks and flowering bushes of all kinds and grass that looked like green velvet, it was so beautifully kept. I stayed at the top so I could somersault down the rolling hill into the gardens. How I loved doing this! I would somersault down, then run back up the steps and somersault down again over and over until I was completely exhausted. My dress by this time was covered in small pieces of newly-mown grass and so was my hair.....and that lovely clean smell of grass! I love it to this day.....and to this day newly-mown grass brings back memories of the Rock Garden. When it started to get dark we would take the tram back to the stop closest to Dundonald Street and walk back from there. Sometimes Dad, Ian and Heather would be waiting for us, and sometimes we waited for them to arrive, the grown-ups sitting in the rocking chairs on the verandah.

These are some vivid childhood memories that remain clearly in my mind and form part of who I am today.

First Visit to England

1957

Here I am, just 18, on board a big tourist liner starting a trip to England. How wonderful, how frightening, how absolutely thrilling to be going to England for the first time, and on my own too. More or less anyway. Mum and Dad, as parents will, made sure that a friend of theirs was also traveling on the ship... Aunt Sally Hardy whose husband Uncle Fred was my godfather. We were to have adjoining cabins.

I was born and bred in Trinidad and up to now the only part of the world I'd visited was the West Indies. My parents were also born in the West Indies of Scottish, French, Italian and English ancestors...and here I was going to the United Kingdom to see what it was really like for myself.

I was sad to say goodbye to Mum and Dad yet felt very daring to be doing something on my own for the first time. We all had a drink in the bar and then the horn sounded for all visitors to leave and after hugs and kisses and me shedding a few tears Mum and Dad left the ship and I decided to go down to the cabin to unpack.

I was disappointed in my cabin which was a tiny box of a thing. Although I was traveling first class I was in one of the less expensive cabins and it couldn't have been smaller. There was just enough room for one person to stand up and move around in it. I managed to balance one suitcase on the small chair that only just fitted into the minute space and had just opened it when it turned upside down!

All my new things scattered on the floor and a box of powder flew open and the cabin was full of clouds of powder for some seconds before it finally settled over everything! I looked despairingly at the

Gillie in 1957

confusion, then looked out of the porthole in time to see the dock receding into the distance and the figures of my beloved parents waving to a daughter they could not see but were already worrying about no doubt...

..I sat on the narrow bunk and cried; then I pulled myself together, tidied up the confusion and lay back on the bunk listening to the muffled sounds of the ship's engines and wondering what would happen next.....

Well, Aunt Sally came in and said she had checked the dinner arrangements and we were to be at the second sitting but at different tables.

I was shown to my table by the Head Waiter and introduced to everyone. An elderly Scottish couple were sitting opposite to me; then there was an English bachelor sitting next to me who had boarded the ship in Trinidad also. His name was Freddie and he looked about mid-thirties, swarthy and attractive although not handsome feature to feature. He was going home on leave from his work in the oilfields. A girl was sitting at the head of the table who was introduced to me as the Purser, she would have been nice looking if she could have lost some weight. At the other end sat a *very* beautiful woman. She also had boarded in Trinidad, the wife of a doctor. Her husband could not leave to come but she said she simply had to spend four months of every year in Europe. She had long brown hair, big brown eyes, a full red mouth and the most beautiful complexion I have ever seen. We did not see much of her; she ate meals with us and then was snatched up by one or other of the officers and spirited away. What amazed me was that Freddie ignored her. Mind you he ignored me as well, and also the Purser (the large lady at the head of the table). The only words the women at the table got from Freddie were the absolute necessities such as 'Good morning', 'Good night', et cetera, otherwise he talked to Mr. MacTaggert, the Scotsman, about ships and boats and tugs and anything that floated on the sea. Sometimes I listened, sometimes I talked to the Purser, sometimes I just sat and ate my dinner and wondered about the Doctor's wife.....so gorgeous, spending four months of each year away from her husband.....I found myself imagining all sorts of stories about her.

One night Freddie turned to me and said, "You look lovely tonight; you dress very well. If you'd put on a bit of weight I'd really fall for you." I was astonished; before I could think what to answer he was back in conversation with Mr. MacTaggert. Actually for all the time I knew Freddie that was the most romantic thing he ever said to me. I have been paid many compliments before and since but I've never forgotten this one because it was so completely foreign to Freddie. Actually they were the first words he addressed to me personally except for the 'Goodnights' and 'Good-days.' After that he would sometimes drop me a word or two during dinner and I felt quite honoured, in spite of myself, to be the only girl at the table to be addressed by Freddie.

One day Aunt Sally introduced me to a girl named Meg O'Shea. Meg was lovely. She was tall and big-boned with literally golden hair. She also had come on board in Trinidad. We became quite friendly and I discovered she had not been well and was going home to England for a rest. She was married to an Irishman who lived and worked in Trinidad. On getting to know her better I realized that she loved her husband very much but all had not been well between them and she had become ill with worry hence the rest at home in England with her parents. Years later I learned that she had returned to Trinidad but they had later separated and divorced and she had gone back to England for good. However I knew nothing of this at the time. Meg knew Freddy casually in Trinidad and we all got together that night for the Disguise Ball. I went as an artist in my black jeans, red shirt and black beret and a paintbrush in my hand. I can't remember what Meg went as and Freddy came to my cabin to ask if he could borrow my housecoat and he went in that! Of course it couldn't begin to fit him..his arms and shoulders couldn't get into it so he had it around his neck like a shawl! He looked so funny that I burst out laughing.....but really Meg and I were bored to tears. Freddy and another man who joined us didn't dance so we just sat there and watched everyone dancing and eventually, with sleep rapidly overcoming me, I excused myself and went to my cabin. I don't think Meg was far behind.

Things began getting boring for me as the days went by. Except for Meg there were no young people around to be friends with. Freddy and his pal spent all day playing cards. I wandered around the pool often stopping to gaze over the side at the tourist class passengers. They made me wish I hadn't been booked first class. They were all young and seemed to be having lots of fun. The result of being bored and lack of young company was that I started flirting with the young steward who served our table. He was good-looking and about my age (18) and we began to have long conversations during mealtimes and sometimes afterwards I'd stay at table a little longer and we'd chat away. His name was Ron and he was very nice. I noticed Freddy did not approve at all and would scowl darkly whenever I talked to Ron at dinner. Sometimes Freddy would wait for me and escort me out possessively after dinner only to disappear once we were outside without saying a word. He really was an odd one!

The U.K. with all its long heard about treasures and excitements was coming nearer and nearer. We were now only three days away from England and would be stopping at Le Havre for eight hours . Ron had asked me to go ashore with him and I was looking forward to it tremendously. Meg had become friendly with a very nice Army Officer and we were to make it a foursome....only it became a fivesome!!

Freddy, without saying a word to any of us beforehand, turned up at the docks and joined us and he never let Ron and I out of his sight for the whole time. Meg and her Army Officer decided to go sight seeing by bus, but Ron and I wanted to go up the little railway that went to the top of the hill. Freddy came too.

What Freddy was up to I can't imagine.....he seemed to have appointed himself my guardian and protector. If he'd been interested in me romantically he'd had plenty of time to show me in some way but he'd done nothing at all and I neither wanted or needed protection. You'd have thought that poor Ron was an old roué intent on seducing me. He was actually very shy and it took all his courage to hold my hand when we were sitting in the taxi on the way back to the ship (with Freddy sitting stolidly in front)!

The following day I felt very squeamish and stayed in my cabin most of the day. Meg came in to see me bringing me 'anything I can do?' messages from Freddy and Ron and I began to feel quite sad that I would be parting from them all on the following day. That night we had our last dinner together.

Mr. McTaggert asked Freddy what he was going to do for his holidays. Freddy said he was going to fish, have pints in the 'local' and play darts and then with a wink in his eye he added, 'and have some cuddles with the Vicar's daughter.'

That night I packed until late and I remember Aunt Sally waking me up early in the morning.....and there was England..... with all the English houses, so much alike, with smoke coming from the chimneys and washing blowing in the breeze. The ship hadn't yet docked, but was moving very slowly. I remember a mad rush of passports and boat trains and catching a last glimpse of Meg at Paddington Station. She introduced me to her mother and we made great promises to write but never did.

Freddy appeared out of the mass of people and shook my hand and said he hoped to see me again and was I sure I'd be alright in London and would someone be with me and did I know where to go. You'd think I was a terrified orphan standing there....

I reassured him on everything and bade him an affectionate goodbye with a kiss on the cheek. I must say that after the departure of this last familiar face I was very glad that Mum and Dad had made sure I was traveling with an old family friend. I was so glad to have Aunt Sally at my side in the midst of all these strange, rushing people busily calling for porters.

Aunt Sally called for a taxi to take us to the Trevose Hotel where we were staying. As we settled in the taxi and I looked towards our ship I saw Freddy standing in the distance, waving. I opened the taxi window and waved my hand until we were lost in the other traffic and I could no longer see him. It was only then that I remembered that I didn't even know Freddy's last name and felt a tinge of sadness. I never did see Freddy again.

A Lamb Called Agatha

It was 1972 and my husband Doug was managing a lovely hotel on the island of Grenada called The Riviera Hotel. The Riviera was composed of a number of cottages set in a beautiful tropical garden on Grand Anse Beach. The entrance to the hotel was at the top of the gardens with the Reception and dining area looking out across the gardens and cottages to the beach. Our house was also in the gardens to one side of the cottages. At the top of the garden was a large pond full of lilies. After my husband took over the management of The Riviera, he built an open wooden bar out across the pond with lights on all sides lighting up the pond and lilies. Our guests would sit there in the evenings for a drink before dinner. It was most attractive and my husband received many compliments for his idea in the building of it.

We also had a Beach Bar for guests relaxing during the day. It was during the height of our busy season. The hotel was full and in the evening to help my husband I would join certain guests for dinner.....usually they were the guests who'd been with us for a week or longer; also Doug held a cocktail party for all the guests once a week when I would join him and meet everyone.

One evening when I was dressed to go out to the hotel for dinner, our daughter Cathy, aged five, was in her nightie and our son Skene who was eighteen months and also dressed for bed— the three of us were waiting for our baby-sitter Matrina to come. She was usually early but tonight she arrived about ten minutes late looking tired and a bit harassed..

"Evening Matrina, everything okay?" I asked. She told me she felt very tired as she'd had a busy day at home and on top of

37

everything else her sheep had given birth to twins that morning, one black and white, the other one totally black and the sheep had cast aside the black lamb, refusing to have anything to do with her. Matrina went on to ask me if she could have one of Skene's old bottles and a nipple so she could try and feed the baby lamb when she got home.....

I immediately went to look for one and as my hand found one at the back of the kitchen cupboard my heart went out to that little lamb who'd had no comfort or nutrition since she'd been born early this morning and to the tired look on Matrina's face and I turned and asked Matrina if she'd like us to look after the little lamb for her. Matrina looked very relieved and said she would like that very much.

I rang my husband Doug, told him the story and why I would not be up for dinner this evening; then Matrina, Cathy, Skene and I got into our car and I drove the couple of miles to the Village where Matrina lived, and we collected her little lamb and brought her home with us. She was too weak to stand but drank about half the bottle of milk we had prepared for her and then fell sound asleep in the cardboard box lined with a soft towel that we had ready for her.

Then we all sat around the kitchen table trying to decide a name for her.....lots of names went back and forth when suddenly I found myself standing up and saying very clearly in a definite tone of voice, "I want to call her Agatha."....and at the same time feeling quite astonished at myself. Matrina, Cathy and Skene all accepted the name without question, but later that evening when Doug came home and was asking why I had called her Agatha I told him I really did not know and I thought I would change the name in the morning.....but the following morning Cathy was in the kitchen with the lamb before me, hugging her and calling her 'Agatha', and the name stayed.

As the days and weeks passed Agatha grew and became a beloved family pet. She loved us and if we went out she would come running and jumping to meet us when we returned along with our little Boston Terrier 'Cutie.' Everyone loved her except perhaps for our Head Gardner who complained to me that she was eating all the hibiscus flowers!.....so I encouraged him to let the hibiscus grow higher where Agatha could not reach them and just leave a few low bushes here and there.....sometimes I would notice yellow pollen all around her face and grab a damp cloth to clean it off hoping that the gardener hadn't noticed it first!

Agatha must have been about two and a half months old when, one Saturday morning I decided to take the children down to the beach. Doug was busy up at the hotel and could not come.....I was walking down the main hotel garden path to the beach holding Cathy's hand on one side and Skene's on the other with our little dog Cutie running in front of us and beside him our beautiful lamb running and jumping, when one of our guests came out onto his balcony and called out, "Mrs. Howie, Mrs. Howie;" I stopped and the children and I and our two pets walked over to his room (Agatha eating a few hibiscus on the way)!

He said, "Mrs. Howie, how lovely it is to see that little lamb with you.....what is her name?" I said, "Well.....her name is Agatha.".... and he smiled and said, "That is a wonderful name for her, Saint Agatha will be pleased." I didn't know what to say and must have stood there looking a bit puzzled. He said, "Didn't you know there was a Saint Agatha?" and I admitted that I did not know this. Then he said, "wait a minute," and turned and went back into his room and came back out with something in his hand and handed it to me. It was a holy picture of the statue of a saint and beside her was a little black lamb; underneath it said, 'Saint Agatha' and her symbol a black lamb.

I felt quite astonished and very touched, thanked him very much and turned back towards our house with the children and our pets to put the picture in my prayer book.....it wasn't until later that evening that I took the picture out of my prayer book to look at it again and read in smaller print underneath, 'Feast Day Feb. 5th and felt my heart beating as I remembered our lamb had been born in February. I looked for my diary and there it was, " Feb. 5th 1972 : Today we have a new pet.....a lovely black lamb born this morning" ...... And I go on to describe how this came about.

How do you explain these things? I couldn't then and I can't now; I only know that when I suddenly made that definite decision to call her 'Agatha' I astonished myself and now there seemed to be a reason.....And slowly over the years more and more things fitted together—

Our guest who gave me the picture turned out to be a Jesuit Priest, his full title being "Dr. Timothy E. Toohig, S.J., On assignment with the U.S.A. Department of Energy, overseeing the U.S.A. Program in High Energy Physics."

Doug and I became good friends with him and kept in touch over the years. In January 2001 he sent us a beautiful paper he had written titled "Physics Research: Search For God" which we will always treasure. [1]

On his covering letter to his Paper he writes: "Gillie, In answer to your question. This is a paper I gave at Loyola University in New Orleans during the year. Blessings, Timothy Toohig, S.J."

We were very sad in 2002 when we heard that he had died. It is a friendship we will always treasure and it was Agatha who put us in touch with each other.

As the years passed I continued to ask myself questions about our extraordinary little lamb and the naming of her and more answers came into view.

Sometime in the 1980's after living for seven years in Gairloch (in the Highlands of Scotland where Doug managed The Gairloch Sands Hotel) we returned to live in our family home in Antigua. In Antigua I became friendly with two beautiful Sisters of Saint Clare, Sister Kathleen and Sister Margaret, who lived and worked amongst the poor and before they left Antigua they gave me a very special Prayer Book—"Christian Prayer—The Liturgy Of The Hours"—and in it there is a short account of Saint Agatha:

"February 5th, AGATHA Virgin and Martyr. Agatha died as a martyr in the persecution of Decius in the year AD 251. She was of a rich and illustrious family and was born and died in *Catania*, Sicily. She is the Patron Saint of Sicily and is also honoured as Patroness of Malta.."....and earlier last year (2014) on reading our Family Tree I see that Francesca my great-great-great grandmother was born in *Catania* in Sicily and her full name is Francesca Agatha Gaetana of the House of San Guiliano, daughter of the Marchese di San Guiliano. [2] What a wonderful thing the mystery of life is!

"Omnipotence and infinite wisdom are not to be caught off balance by coincidence or accident. Chance is not God's rival but His instrument in the interlocking pattern of nature's activity."

Saint Thomas Aquinas

"It is a wonderful feeling to recognise the unifying features of a complex of phenomena which present themselves as quite unconnected in the direct experience of the senses."

Isaac Newton

Notes:

1 A quote from the beautiful Paper—PHYSICS RESEARCH—SEARCH FOR GOD by Dr. Timothy Toohig, S.J. : ."....Even if by simple introspection, and by making his original transcendental experiences thematic, a person could not individually discover such a transcendental experience of God's self-communication in grace, or could not express it by himself with unambiguous certainty, nevertheless, if this theological and dogmatic interpretation of his transcendental experience is offered to him by the history of revelation and by Christianity, he can recognise his own experience in it....." Dr. Toohig's beautiful Paper offers insights into the reality of God on all levels and is a treasure to possess.

2 Francesca married Edward Dacres Baynes, my great, great, great grandfather in 1818. Edward D. Baynes had a distinguished military career. He saw service with the garrison in Malta and used to spend his leave exploring the beauties of the Mediterranean countries. On one such leave in Sicily he met and subsequently married Francesca Gaetana di San Guiliano daughter of the Marchese di San Guiliano. On August 21st, 1833 he was sent to Jamaica as Special Magistrate to enforce The Abolition of Slavery act. Around 1856 he went with his family to live in Antigua where they lived for the rest of their lives and where they are now buried.

Annie

Annie Benjamin née Sterling
Born May 1901 in English Harbour, Antigua
Died 12th December, 1986 in Cedar Grove, Antigua

August 1983

Annie came today calling "Maaam..." My whole family have a special place in their hearts for Annie—82 years old and still trundling her little cart from Cedar Grove to Hodges Bay. Her cart is full of a variety of vegetables, most of them rotten. I'm sure Annie must get the cast offs that other vendors cannot sell as she is too old now to go down to the wharf to make her selection.

Annie has been selling local fruit and veg in our area for well over twenty years. For years she came with her donkey 'Harris' (Horace) and, at one stage, it was Annie, Harris and Harris's foal. But eventually Harris became too much for Annie to manage and she was given or sold to family and Annie got her little cart.

Annie lives on a pension of EC$35 a month—paid to her as a war widow. Her husband fought in the 1st World War. She has no children of her own and all her brothers and sisters are dead. She had a piece of land in St. Johns which she sold and bought a piece of land in Cedar Grove where she built a one room wooden house. Everyone in Cedar Grove call her 'aunt' Annie as a sign of respect.

Although she had no children she looked after many of her nieces and nephews. Her favourite niece, Mary, married young and had three children. Then Mary's husband decided to go to Aruba where he'd been offered a good job on an oil rig. Within a few days of his arrival in Aruba, he was killed in an explosion on the rig. Mary was notified but by the time she got a passport and got to Aruba her husband was already buried.

Annie and her donkey with Cathy and Skene

Mum with Annie

While still in Aruba, Mary's mother, Annie's sister, died in Antigua of a heart attack. Mary came back to bury her mother. Tragedy struck again when her second husband was killed in a car crash at Friars Hill leaving her penniless with six children. It was then that Annie gave Mary a piece of her land at Cedar Grove and a two room wooden house was built on it for Mary and her six children.

Annie also looked after Mary's brother (her nephew) who had become mentally ill after his mother died. However, he became worse and worse and was put into the mental home. Mary is now dead and her brother is out of the mental home and is trying to get Annie put into Fiennes Institute—the home for old people.

In the last few years the government built a two-room concrete house for Annie to replace her one-room wooden house which was on the verge of collapse and she is proud of her new house. There is no running water or electricity but Annie does not seem to miss these things as she has never had either and I doubt she would be able to pay water and electricity rates. Her water is stored in a rain barrel at the side of the house and cooking is done on her coal pot.

18th June, 1984

Annie came today. She no longer pushes her cart as it is a long way for her to walk and some months ago we told her not to bring us vegetables and fruit but please to visit regularly and we give her a monthly allowance. On the way here she picks different kinds of bush for her bush tea and always gets some limes from our lime tree when it is bearing. She was using an old piece of wood as a walking stick and I replaced it with a nice smooth piece Skene (our son) had in his room. She told us that she has left her house to a nephew who lives in St. Maarten and who has promised to return and give her a good funeral when she dies.

Annie often gives news of people in our area. While she was sitting having her drink of juice she told me that while she was walking past Marsdens house she saw someone clearing the bush in front of the gate (the house has been overgrown and deserted for years) and wanted to ask him if he was Marsden's son—"but mistress I too embarrass to ask the gentleman after what I did. You know one thing I 'fraid too bad is cattle and the way I walk bend over now I suddenly see two cattle hoof in front my eye so I hit out with my stick.....and shout, *"move off! get away from me!"* When I look up I see a gentleman looking down at me. Like he wearing these shoes with a white piece of rubber across the front."....by this time I was laughing and Annie was laughing too.

We found out later that the Marsdens had just returned to Antigua with their son and his wife and are busy putting their house back in shape.

27th June 1984

Annie came today. She still has the good stick of Skenes I gave her.

She told me she had seen the same gentleman by Marsden's house and had apologised to him for the episode last week—"I tell him I too sorry for the way I treat him last week but he must excuse me because I thought he was cattle."

1985

Sometime in late 1985 I started visiting aunt Annie once a month bringing her the family allowance as the walk to our house had become too much for her. I would sit on her sofa (an old car seat) and we always had a chat. Annie loves to tell stories of her childhood.

28th June, 1986

Today I went to see Annie bringing some Ovaltine and her monthly allowance. She told me this story from her childhood in Falmouth, English Harbour.....

"My mother die when I very young and my stepmother she don't treat us good atall so all the children leave home, but I too young to leave so I stay right there and my father he don't pay no attention.

One day my brother pay me a visit and when he go back to where he was staying he tell my older brother, 'You better go and take Annie away or she go die where she is.' My older brother came down to English Harbour and he take me back with him to my Aunty who live by where the old cemetery used to be. A few of my brothers and sisters already were staying with she. (The old cemetery was by the entrance to Deep Water Harbour.)

Every morning before coal pot light Aunty get we down on we knee on the floor and she open the Bible and read to us. She tell we, 'All of you who understand what I am reading—remember—and if you don't understand yet—listen—because this is the word of God I am reading.' And every night before we lay down we head we get down on knee again and listen as Aunty read God's word and try to remember.

Also we say the Our Father together.

One day my Father came to take me back with him to English Harbour, but I do not want to go back and Aunty would not let him take me. She say I am not going from her house and my Father tell she he going to bring Police for she.

Well, some time after that my Father come back with two Police to take me back with him. I hang on to Aunty dress while the Police ask she question after question and then they bring out a big book with lines and give Aunty a pen and she have to write in plenty different parts of this book.

Then the Police tell my Father that he cannot take me ' because the child want to stay with she Aunty,' and my Aunty has signed on to take care of me.

Well, time pass and one day when I reach about twelve years old, a man came up from English Harbour to tell us that my Father is dying and he wish to see his children to ask forgiveness before he dies.

My aunt sit in front of me and she tell me that all this time she would not let my Father have me because he treat me too bad, but now the time has come when I must go and see my Father.

She help me to dress in my church clothes and tell me the way to English Harbour is not difficult—that once I get to the gates of St.John's, the road goes in a straight line from there. I leave home about twelve o'clock. Sometimes I running, sometimes I walking, and I reach English Harbour about five o'clock.

My Father was lying there in his house. His woman was not with him—she was in the village talking with friends. He hold my hand and start to cry and ask if I was really Annie his daughter. I tell him yes. He say he want to ask my forgiveness and the forgiveness of all his children for the way he treat us when we were very young —

"Annie, do you forgive me?" he ask.

"Yes Father I forgive you," I say to him.

Then he sigh and roll over on his side and he say, "Annie, get a cloth and clean your Father."

Poor man, I lift his shirt and I see his body covered in poops. I get a bowl, fill it with water from the barrel outside and with a piece of cloth I find in the house I wash down his body and take away his shirt to wash.

I stay with him until he die which was the next week."

31st August, 1986

Today I went to see Annie with her allowance and a few things —Ovaltine, sardines, condensed milk, corn beef, biscuits, limes and some dog food for her dog. Annie has not been feeling well these past few weeks—the cloudy weather affects her arthritis. She says the doctor gave her a prescription but the Dispensary has none at this time.

Her great nephew came in to see her while I was there. His name is Gavin.

I stayed with Annie for a while and Annie talked to me about her husband, Harry Benjamin, who was born in Sea View Farm. His mother and father were married but his father did not spend much time at home.

When he was in his teens he got into trouble with his church Minister, a Moravian, who was very strict with the young people and if he did not approve of the way they were behaving during the week he would admonish them in his Sunday sermon and sometimes they would have to stay in after Service for a caning with 'the big stick.'

The church Minister was an Antiguan, born in New Winthropes and sent to Sea View Farm after he was ordained.

Mrs. Benjamin was very upset when her son was given a caning one Sunday and said, "No one ever going to beat my picnee again."

She packed a bag for him and sent him to work on the boats so that he could see the world.

Harry went to sea and was in Panama when the 1st World War started. He was asked to join the British Army and his mother received papers from the War Office asking permission for her son to sign on. She signed the papers and sent them back, feeling very proud of Harry.

By then she was high up in the Moravian Church and everyone knew her as 'Ma Pinch.'

So Harry Benjamin joined the British Army and fought for them in the 1st World War.

Annie had not yet met him. She was only seventeen in 1918 when Victory was declared and says she will never forget the day.....

They woke up to Church Bells ringing everywhere—clang a lang, ring a ding, and when they went outside they saw a car driving by with its horn blowing..."In those days there was only a very few cars in Antigua and no 'planes atall and yet on this day I think all the cars in Antigua drive into St. John's with horn blowing and all the while church bells ringing —clang a lang, ring a ding.

Everybody gather in the streets to find out what is happening and then someone came running up the street shouting to all of us, *"we done win the war,"* and we all felt excited and happy.

The celebrations continued throughout the day and that night there was a big fireworks display on Otto's Hill (now Michael's Mount). Everyone had gathered to see the fireworks and the display started well with all eyes looking into the sky at the showers of stars—when suddenly a rocket misfired into the huge box containing all the fireworks and there was a loud explosion with all the rockets taking off in different directions.

Many people were badly burnt, among them Annie. She spent a month in hospital and then went home, but it took her over a year to recover completely and the scars were with her for the rest of her life.

.......It was a couple of years later that Annie met Harry Benjamin when he came back to Antigua and joined the Police Force. They fell in love and got married, but she says Harry was not a good husband to her...a real roamer who 'lived out' with other women and did not support her in any way.

Eventually she left him and went back to her aunt where she made a living by making coal pots and selling them.

One day she got a message telling her to come to the hospital because her husband was ill. He'd had a stroke while riding on his donkey.

Annie went to the hospital to see him but says, "He was already travelling to death and did not recognise me." He died a few days later.

Although he had a house and land it was taken over by his parents and Annie got nothing. His parents told Annie that he had 'drunk out' his house and land.

21st November, 1986

Annie is now bedridden and she is dying. I feel depressed and sad over the poverty she has lived in all her life and the hardships she's endured.....but I also realise that Annie has accomplished alot with what she had.....she has never been a morose person and must have experienced many happy times but now when I visit her with some basic things to make life easier I still feel very helpless in this little house with no furniture except a bed, two small tables heaped up with odd bottles, pieces of cloth and this, that and the other, and the old car seat with broken springs. The walls are blackened from months of cooking inside the house on her coal pot and there are no curtains; an old, torn dress covers part of the window.

I know Annie does not want to move from the house she loves so much but she is now helpless and there is never anyone here when I visit and everything is soiled. I do not know where to start. I have given her neighbour, Ruby, some gifts for herself and asked her at the same time if she could visit Annie three times a day for me, just to give her a drink and light the kerosene lamp at night and we have sent a message to her family (nephews and nieces) to ask if we can bring in some members of the St. Vincent de Paul Society to help us clean the house and bathe Annie. I see alot of soiled clothes piled up in different bundles on the floor but do not want to remove them in case among the different bundles may be some treasured possessions of Annie.

24th November, 1986

I visited Annie today to find there had been a complete transformation in her house. I could hardly believe my eyes. The house had been swept and scrubbed; all the soiled bundles of clothes had disappeared and now there was a lovely old hat/coat Stand in the corner and hanging on it was an umbrella and a ladies coat. The old car seat was still against the wall but now it was covered with a clean bedspread and even had a cushion placed on it; against the other wall was one of Annie's small carved wooden tables with a tin of Ovaltine and an enamel cup on it.

I went into Annie's room. Annie was lying on her side in bed and did not seem to recognise me. She was murmuring to herself. Her bed (an old four-poster) had been made up with clean linen and a clean cotton blanket (one that Mum gave Annie years ago) was tucked in over her feet. There was a clean pillow-case on her pillow. Annie herself looked washed and clean. For the first time there were curtains over the bedroom windows. The curtains were blowing in the breeze and sunlight came through the window and across the edge of the bed. Beside the bed was the other wooden table and on it was a thermos of hot Ovaltine and a covered water container with a clean enamel cup beside it.

I sat on the bed beside Annie and said a prayer of thanks while I held her hand and looked at our old friend. She seemed thirsty so I opened a packet of apple juice, put a straw in it and Annie drank almost all of it. She can no longer eat anything solid.

I talked to Annie for a while and although she did not talk her eyes seemed to understand. I told her how much all her friends in Hodges Bay loved her and missed her and how we all remembered her coming to see us with 'Harris' and how each week we'd looked forward to her arrival... and Annie smiled... the first smile I'd seen in a long time. I'd brought some limes with me as I remembered how Annie loved limes and always picked a few from our tree when she came to see us. When she saw the limes she pointed to them and then to her head; so I rubbed her head gently with one half of a lime.

While I was still there Annie's great niece came in to check on her and her neighbour told me that Annie's parish priest was coming to give her communion the next day. Annie is Church of England.

CONCLUSION

I never saw Annie again, but early in the morning of December 12th, I dreamt that Mum had come with me to visit Annie and with us had come a man who was a stranger to me. I tried to see him clearly because in my dream I was puzzled as to why he was with us but his face always seemed turned away from me.

Mum and I and this stranger went into the house and there, standing in front of us, was Annie, dressed in a bright flowered dress and looking very well. Her face had filled out and she was smiling.

Mum held my arm and said, "Gillie, Annie is getting better."

Then Annie walked past us, through the front door, down the steps, opened her gate and started walking down the road without looking back.

I half woke up, turned over and said to myself, "What a relief... Annie is getting better."

On the day of the funeral I was ill with a bad stomach pain and could not attend but heard that it was very well attended and the nephew to whom she'd left the house had arrived from St. Maarten with two lovely wreaths and had made all the funeral arrangements and all her nieces and nephews were there.

Memories of an Old Antiguan

As related to Gillian Howie during several conversations in 1997

Reuben was born at Cassada Gardens in the month of October 1924. He cannot remember the exact day. His mother's name was Sarah married to John Carr an overseer on the estate. His mother worked in the grounds of the estate which belonged to Moody-Stuart and was part of Syndicate Estates Limited.

1924–1936

CASSADA GARDENS

Reuben has happy memories of his childhood. He remembers running about and playing with the other children born on the estate. "I remember all the sugar cane standing high and sometimes when some break off, the Manager—Mr. Spencer—did give it to us, and SO we love it.

I remember that every Sunday we have Sunday School on the estate. A big lady teach us. I forget she name now, but she very nice. I look forward to Sunday School; and on the big festivity like Christmas and so, we have a wonderful time. The Manager see that all the children have a treat; it was so good you hear; and it was only for we born on the estate; they allow nobody else.

One day my mother said to me, 'Reuben I am going to teach you this lesson I have on this piece of paper and you must learn it well now, because I am going to get you confirmed,' and we sit down and we read this lesson word after word and time after time;

and I learn it well you hear. I have to say the lesson every Sunday at Sunday School, and so it go on; every week my mother teach me a lesson and we say it together until we sure I have every word and you can be sure come time for Sunday School I know my lesson. And so the day come when it was Confirmation Exam and only those children, *those* children who could say their lesson, could pass for Confirmation and you know I pass, yes, I pass, and on Confirmation Day my mother have some special clothes for me, and *yes*, I get confirm in The *big church* and *now* I become a child of God. That is what they say you know, yes that is what they tell me.

ST. JOHN'S BOYS SCHOOL

While I was still a small person we live on the hill at Cassada Gardens and I go to school at St. John's Boys School. Many small people were at that school. Mr. Kirnon was the Headmaster. He was a short, heavy man. A good man and strict as well; Furthermore he was Inspector of Schools as well; and you know The St.John's Boys School name after him now? Now it is The T.N. Kirnon School.

To the east of the St. John's Boys School was The Antigua Grammar School and to the east of The Grammar School was Lady Nugent Cemetery. When we leave school in the afternoon no one walk slow past Lady Nugent, everyone run past there FAST, especially the girls, but in truth the boys well run fast themselves. Every day was some new story about the ghost by Lady Nugent Cemetery.

Well now the time come when I leave St. John's Boys School and go to the Cedar Grove School but that is another story."

THE BIG HURRICANE

"I remember now what made us move from Cassada Gardens. It was that big, big, hurricane. That hurricane was big you hear. It take away most people roof and then the house blow away too. I living with my mother, father and grandmother up at Cassada and when the roof blow off it was nearly dark already, about six o'clock.

We all run out of the house and although we try to stay together the wind blow us off in different directions. Me and my grandmother manage to stay together. We get to a house which still has a roof but in no time that roof gone too and the same thing happen again, everybody run out the house and go in different direction, but my grandmother and me, we stay together. By this time it was dark and the wind was terrible. We come to a very big tree and we sit down underneath bunching up against each other. The hurricane seem to last forever. Even when it get light the wind still strong and we frighten, yes we really frighten but we could see no place to go, so we stay bunch up there until they (my mother and father) find us about five o'clock in the afternoon.

CEDAR VALLEY

Well, after this hurricane there was no place to live at Cassada Gardens, so they move my father to Cedar Valley where he was groom for Moody-Stuart horses. Moody-Stuart have horses you know and he keep them at Cedar Valley. I move with my father to Cedar Valley and my mother and grandmother move to Barnes Hill. In those days I spend my time between Cedar Valley and Barnes Hill. Weekday at my father in Cedar Valley and weekend at my mother in Barnes Hill.

Cedar Valley where my father and me live now was a sugar estate too. Everywhere you look was sugar. Longfords was sugar, all going up by Shaeffler was sugar. The Manager at Longfords was Mr. Abbott. The Manager at Cedar Valley was Mr. McFarlane. Sometimes Mr. McFarlane would drive us into St. John's in his car to do shopping. This was 'specially 'round Christmas time.

And at Cedar Valley, the same as Cassada Gardens, we have Sunday School every Sunday in a big house they have there. I always did love Sunday School.

Down in Cedar Valley is a lovely pond. A big pond you hear, and is also another pond on the estate, a small one. But this big pond really nice and when the pond purge it clear and fresh. You could see right down. I remember when I feel thirst I would lie down on my stomach so, my face in the pond and drink my belly full. The water taste too sweet.

Many people use the pond for water. They would come with bucket, two, three, four bucket. They use it for everything, to wash clothes, to wash theyself, for the animals, because you know in them days we have no pipe water.

Now when we have drought is another thing. The pond would be low, low, and just damp at the bottom. The government would send a boat called 'tug' to Dominica and it come back full of fresh water. Then the water go into these tank which trucks did bring for us in Cedar Valley and the people up at Barnes Hill. Everybody waiting with their bucket for when the truck come.

In them days when the first rain come people run out they house and stand in the rain with hand lift up high over they head to catch the water from the sky, laughing, and we know too the ponds would fill."

Reuben told me this morning some more of his memories while living with his father at Cedar Valley where his father was groom for Moody-Stuarts horses. "My father was good with those horses you hear and Mr. Moody-Stuart made my father Head Groom, and there I was, a small person, but working with my father all the while.

I did love those horses too bad; don't mind they so big; they did stand tall above me so that I have to look up from underneath them, and they beautiful, they really beautiful. Mr. Moody-Stuart make sure his horses are the best. And I could ride them too and no horse ever throw me, don't mind I so small. People would tell my father 'You better watch out. That boy go fall,' and my father would say, 'You don't worry. He can hold that horse.' Furthermore those horses know me well because I with them every day. I help my father feed them and I help him keep them clean so they shine and furthermore I ride them almost every day so they can exercise.

Another thing my father tell me was, 'Keep your knee close in so they touch the horse on both side and anytime the horse look to throw you, you just hold onto the mane,' and it always work.

Mr. Moody-Stuart often want to inspect his estates. On that day he always tell my father which horse he want to ride. My father would ride one horse and I would ride the next horse from Cedar Valley to Cassada Gardens. From there Moody-Stuart and another man would get on the horses and go to inspect the estates. Sometimes they gone for a whole day. When they get back my father and myself give the horse water and then we ride them back to Cedar Valley.

Other time Mr. Moody-Stuart tell my father his two daughters (and sometimes it was his three daughters) want to go riding and my father must take them through the estate. My father would ride with them to show them everything. He also choose which horse the girls must ride.

HORSERACING

Another thing was when they had the races. In them days I tell you the Race Course look good you hear. It was two story. The white people sit in the top stand and the high up black people in the bottom stand. The people who did not pay to come in have a 'sway' on top the hill so they could watch the races and food and thing all around—but my father and me, we right inside there with the horse and the jockey and we see the race from the front. The jockey look too nice. They wear bright red jacket and shirt that look like draught board with big different colour square; and they trousers now— they trousers buffed out at the side and they wear boots all lace up and when they up on the horse they foot go into the stirrup iron. The stirrup iron high up when they racing. And the jockey always wear cap and a thing like goggles.

In them days they does have a 'straight' leading up *straight* from the powerhouse. They does have this long stretch before the circle start and you can stand up and see everything when the horse coming up the 'straight'; it was easier for betting then; and you know Spencer? Well is Spencer father use to ride in the old days; and listen to me, he was a good jockey you hear.

I tell you the races in those days was a big, big thing. I grow up with horses and I like them all my life.

CEDAR GROVE SCHOOL

Well, you know it is when I go to live with my father at Cedar Valley that I change schools. Now I have to go to the Cedar Grove Primary School. It was three boys from Cedar Valley and about six girls who go to Cedar Grove School.

The school is one big room, not different classroom, one BIG room and the Headmistress is a Miss Jacob. Well Cedar Grove School not easy you know. Those boys from Cedar Grove like to bully you hear. They bully, bully. And not only the boys, is the girls too. One time I remember a big fist and cuff fight with two girls; one is from Cedar Valley, the other one is from Cedar Grove. This fight happen during break. Well, at the close down time what you think happen? A woman, a mother from Cedar Grove, does run into the school ground and give the Cedar Valley girl ONE cuff! Her eye swell up after that. I tell you some of them Cedar Grove people bad you hear; and that is not the end you know.

What you think happen next day? Next day the mother from Cedar Valley arrive at Cedar Grove School with she frying pan in she hand shoutin' for the mother from Cedar Grove. People run to tell the mother from Cedar Grove and she come running out she house with saucepan in hand. *Well!* They start one fight there—is mostly the saucepan and frying pan hittin' but other time they hit each other too. People gather 'round taking sides and they encourage them to go on with the fight. The Headmistress come out and bring all the children back inside the school and she call the Police. Well, the Police arrive and when the women don't listen to them they put the women in handcuff and take them down to the Police Station. That was a thing!

We did have our lunch in a house in Cedar Grove. We bring our own food and this nice woman cook it for all a we. And you know something? Don't mind some did bring small amount and some bring more, when it time for lunch everyone get the same and it always taste good.

When school finish in the afternoon we three boys from Cedar Valley wait on the girls because we always walk home together with them. That way we know all the girls reach home safe.

Another thing in Cedar Valley they let my father use a piece of ground to grow his own provision and he make his own charcoal and I help with that too, we cut and burn the wood to make charcoal. In those days everybody have coal pot and you know the food cook on coal pot taste better than food cook anywhere else. Them inside stove and so, the food don't taste the way food on coal pot taste. After we burn the wood we load two baskets with the charcoal. My father have a donkey and these donkey a big help; they could carry heavy load you hear. The donkey carry the two basket of coal and we walk with him and that way we get the coal back to our house.

That was years gone by and the stables at Cedar Valley gone now, long since, and as for the Plantation House, only the buff remain where it was. The road up to the Plantation House still there but the place where the Plantation House stand is only the buff remain and all around is cossy and bush. The house build on a rise, a nice place.

Today while Reuben and I were chatting I asked him what he had done after he left school.

1936–1981

SUGAR, MOODY-STUART & THE OLD MAN

"Well after I leave school I work in the sugar industry. Yes, it was at Cassada Gardens when it belong to Syndicate Estates. I was young then and they want a boy to work one of those plow. They want a boy to sit on the back of the tractor and pull a rope and when you pull that rope that thing drop and it make the farrow straight where they plant the cane and that is how cane grow.

And furthermore I see the men plant the cane too. They put down the pieces of cane like so—two piece, two piece—each one face the other one in the farrow. They dig the place for each cane with a pick. When they finish, then they would put the mold.

But I forget to say—before the men plant the cane they did have some ladies with big basket fill up with sugar-cane plant and they drop the cane plant one, one, one, along the farrow and then when the men come with they pick they just start to plant. These ladies not young girls you know but *big*, *big*, ladies and when they start to drop they could drop a whole field in one day. In them days when you going into St. John's and you see some men line up by the side of the road, you say, 'Ah! They go plant cane today.' I work in the sugar a few years well.

And then the time come when Mr. Vere Cornwall Bird come in and he talk about Union and he FORM the Union. The Union speak to Moody-Stuart for more pay for the workers and Moody-Stuart say no—so the Union tell we, we must stop work for two weeks, we must strike, and up to the last man agree with the Union. And we survive, yes we survive, for in them days the people does eat widdy widdy bush and we survive on that for two weeks until the strike end.

You see Moody-Stuart and them always in conflict with the Union and in them days the money be very small you know and because of the Union we get more. Moody-Stuart have a son who come and run The Syndicate after Moody-Stuart has retire and gone home, and the son want to run The Syndicate how he like and nothing go so, and everything running flat now because different Manager and different people do this and some do that, and by then The Syndicate mash up and the Government buy it over.

By this time Mr. V.C. Bird was Premier and soon we start to change over to Independence and The Queen come down and then our Old Man move from Premier to Prime Minister. Our Old Man do alot in Antigua you know because in my small days there be no Secondary school and so; yes, the people much better off now.

The big people, my mother, I always hear she talk about Bird, Bird, Bird. They always talk about the Old Man. They love him you hear. And look at all the things Bird did.

In those days I was with my mother up at Barnes Hill most days. I remember when the Government say they going to build house for people in need. They ask my mother and she say to build one in my name. At that time we live in a one-way house, you go in one door the bed was there and you go out the next door and you was outside again. A one-way house.

The house I live in now the Government build. It is a concrete house and have two room. We have to pay a little every month but now all the money paid and the house belong to me. It go through alot of hurricane you hear and it still standing. I plant a hedge in front the house and the yard I like to see clean and tidy. I have a big water-barrel, I have electricity and I have television. It is a good house.

THE AMERICANS COME

Well, I must be 'roun seventeen years when I hear people talking 'bout the war. I remember when the Americans come to Antigua.

Down by High Point there we all run to see this enormous ship, it BIG you hear and it have a flat bottom. We have to bend ourselves over to look inside this ship and the top was high up you hear. It was full up with cars, jeep and trucks. We love to look in this thing. I remember we never did call them Americans in those days, we call them Yankees. And you know what? The Yankees every night give us a film show from this very ship. They would put up this big screen and we could watch it from the jetty.

Well, people seem to come from everywhere, young, old, and we all gather on the jetty. Me, I was a young man but I still find people taller than me everywhere; but I find something high to climb upon from where I could see the picture. It was the first time in my life that I see a film show.

I remember too when we all live in the barracks at the Base. Yes, the men who did live there had gone home to America—it was after another hurricane and again all the house went and the Yankees let us live in the barracks. I live there with my mother and grandmother. One barracks was by the filtration plant and one was higher up.

I live in the barracks by the filtration plant which was the one for married people and children and the one higher up—well, I TELL you, the Antiguans who live there were bad you hear? They make noise all night and they gamble too; but where I was with my mother it was quiet. We did everything there. We cook on coal pots to the west because too much wind on the east side; and there was a shop there too. Yes, a lady run a shop by the Exchange and we could buy what we need from there every day.

But some of those Yankees bad you know. In them days we don't see gun in Antigua. You don't even see police with gun. But the Yankees well have gun, and you know what happen? On the Base there they have big storerooms with alot of thing inside and some Antiguans would burgle. On this night they catch two men doing a burgle and they shoot them! That was a thing! By this time we was back up in Barnes Hill and my mother tell me not to go down by the Base again because those Yankees bad and they have gun.

LESSONS

I remember too aroun' that time some of my friends did smoke you know and I decide to try it. I excited you hear; but when I try it I start to choke and I say 'TALL! Me and cigarette never mix since that day; and when you come to drink I could remember when I was a young boy I hear laughing and shouting down the road and I run down to see what happen. A man I know lying down across the middle of the road. He drunk, drunk you hear—drunk until his mind give up. The people were laughing and they pull him over to the side—but his wife not laughing, SHE SHOUTING, I don't even know what words she saying—but I say then I would never spend money on rum to make me feel so. My drink is water, juice too, but water is really my drink.

A BLESSING

My mother Sarah love me very much. She die when I turn nineteen.

I missed my mother. I feel sadness when she leave this world.

Someone tell me, 'Reuben, your mother love you very much. You have been blessed and she leaves a blessing on you.'

I never forget that.

EXPERIMENTAL STATION

At that time I was working at Friars Hill at the Experiment Place where we plant all kind of things. Is agriculture work they do there. They plant pepper, cabbage, corn, cucumber, tomato, and they did provide me with transport. They pass by me in Barnes Hill in the morning and they bring me home in the afternoon. They have a van.

Agriculture does plant a lot in those days. The oil refinery start at that time too."

February 1998

These are some memories of Reuben's youth. He is seventy-four now and still lives an independent life on his own in his home at Barnes Hill. His father died over twenty years ago and Reuben and his half brother gave him a decent funeral.

He keeps in touch with his daughter Mary born out of his love for Lily. Lily died many years ago and Mary has given Reuben three grandsons and now great grand-children.

He has his Savings in a Bank Account and receives a Government Pension.

He still works as gardener for four days a week, the fifth day he gives to his church to keep the grass mown and the grounds tidy. Some years ago when Father Richards was at the Rectory he introduced Reuben to The Mens Fellowship of which he has been a member ever since. When he first joined there were four men and now the membership is about fifteen. They have a meeting every other Tuesday night to study the bible and sing and one Sunday a month they all attend Service together in full uniform. They are also invited to join in prayer and community Mens Fellowship of other churches all over Antigua and on these occasions there is a bus to take them there and back.

His faith and his church are a very important and fulfilling part of Reuben's life.

Faith is not an easy virtue
but in the broad world of
man's total voyage
through time to eternity,
faith is not only a gracious companion, but an essential guide.'

Theodore M. Hesburgh in The Way

The Courage
of Poverty

Amelia and Aaron

Doris rents a three bedroom wooden house on the south side of St. John's.

Doris is a nurse and is comfortably off. The house borders on the street but there is a back yard in which Doris has plans for a garden. Her niece Samantha, who is also a nurse, and two grandsons, live with her.

Further up the street, on the opposite side, lives an old man. They see him every day sitting on the step that borders the pavement, murmuring to himself. He is disheveled and often there is mud on his clothes and feet and he is usually bare-footed. All they can see is the steps, all the rest is high walls of galvanize; they do not even know what is behind the galvanize. Surely there must be a house, but all you can see from outside is the step, the old man and the high galvanize.

One day Doris said to Samantha, "We are both nurses and we should help that old man. Let us pay him a visit and tell him we are his neighbours from down the street and maybe we could see if he needs anything."

That afternoon Doris and Sam walked up the street to visit the old man who was sitting in his usual position on the step with a small stick in his hand, and with this stick he was drawing pictures on the pavement. Of course he was the only one who knew what the pictures were.

"Hello," they said, "we are your neighbours from down the street and we want to know if we can help you in any way, if you have need of anything?"

The old man lifted his head for an instant, waved his hand with the stick in it towards a door cut in the galvanize and then went on with his drawing, talking to himself, once more in a world of his own.

Doris pushed the rusty old galvanize door which scraped along the ground as they opened it, at the same time stepping carefully around the old man.

There in front of them was a good sized plot of land and on it a nice wooden one-bedroom house. The yard was clean and at the back a clothes line had been set up and an old woman, very fat, was standing hanging up her wash. Beside her was an old wash-pan and two buckets of water. A wooden scrubbing board was propped up against the wash-pan. At the end of the yard was a mango tree and several sugar apple trees.

The wash line was tied to the mango tree at one end and to a wooden pole at the other. A short distance from the house was a small wooden out-house. When she saw Doris and Sam the old woman hung the piece of clothing in her hands on the line, wiped her hands on her skirt and came towards them. "God sent you," she said. "I told my husband, God will send someone to help us."

"Yes," Doris said. "In truth we have come to help. What would you wish us to do?" "Come in, come in," she said, at the same time opening the back door of the house. "What I need is one or two dress. It seem I too big for anything the people hand out." In truth she was big, short but wide. She had on one dress over another so that where there were big gaps the other one filled them in.

"My name is Amelia John," she said as they all went into the house, "that man sitting out there is my second husband." Inside the house was clean and well cared for. It was really only two rooms, the living room and the bedroom. In the living room was a small dining table and two chairs and two small armchairs were near the window in the opposite corner. Everything looked clean and well kept. Outside was her kitchen which consisted of a strong wooden table on which rested two coal pots and some well used pots and pans. There were two kerosene lamps in the house and a rain barrel outside situated to catch the water from the roof which was guttered.

"We both wash we own self" she said, "You see he sitting there with mud on he pants but his body clean. His clothes have mud because one of the things he do is sit on the ground here in the backyard and weed. He too old to stoop over now. His name is Aaron—his parents christen him Churchill after an English man but when I meet him he go by the name Aaron. That man too stubborn. He use bad words off he tongue time and again. But I stronger than he you hear and every time I hear those words I bang he and then I bang he again." The old lady had one hand open and the other clenched into a fist and was hitting the fist into her open hand to describe how she kept him in order.

"You know sometimes he leave the house and go down by Market Street and he stand on the pavement at the corner and direct traffic. That one is his favourite thing to do."

"But wait, don't go Miss Doris, come and sit here in this armchair and you too Miss Sam. I want to tell you what it is like to be poor. When you poor you just get poorer and nobody care. They look at you as if you be a piece of rubbish. I not talking about now you know, because *now* I have *means* and people know me, yes people know me now and who you think I speaking about? I speaking about relatives. My relatives come by me now; my cousin does bring coal for me in his truck. No, I have no electricity. What I want with that? I never have electricity in my life and now I can live well without it. I have my lamp. I not going to pay for electricity; and the same go for water. I *not* going to pay for water when I have a standpipe just over there where I could fill my buckets—Aaron fill them for us—and we have we rain barrel too; and the night-soil truck does come at night for our toilet. We put it out in a bucket with a lid and in the morning one of us wash the bucket out and put it back in the 'out-house,' *and* Miss Doris I *own* this house and land. Yes! I pay $12,000 for it when I was age 73. I am 84 years of age now you see me here. I buy me first house at Golden Grove when I turn 66. I did save a little here and a little there every time I work and when I get a job with Government as a cleaner I could save regular and I put it in my Savings Bank and *now* I have good money—since I start my old age pension I get $300.00 a month and then Government call me last year and tell me they put it up to $400.00—so you see—and Aaron he get 300—so now we alright.

But let me tell you Miss Doris about when I was young. When I was young I live in Bolans and my family very poor and I never have a cent; the only treasure you could say I have in my life is education but I too poor to use it. I did go to the school in Bolans and I stay there until I was about 12 years old and then I leave school but I did learn to read and write and since then I always love to read.

Well, time pass and I marry this man. He fooly, fooly, you hear, but what can I do? I want to get marry; and we live in this house—a small house—(Amelia looked around the house she now owned as if it were enormous) and we grow some things on a piece of land my husband—John—use. The only way we get money is when the plants bearing we pack them in bags and take them to market. But it is to get there—sometimes the bus would say no 'we cannot take the bags because there is no room.' Then we just have to walk. We would leave the house about 4 o'clock in the morning.

Later on we get a donkey and then the donkey carry the things and we walk beside it. But sometimes there is nothing to bring to the market and those are the bad times you hear. Sometimes we have something to eat three days in the week, sometimes four; the rest of the time I does cook bush up in the pot and we eat the bush.

You know I have eight children; but only one child still alive. A son. He does drive a truck for Government. The others all gone. My first baby die after about three months. I was feeding him but he die. One night he was alive and when I go to feed him early next morning I realise the baby dead. I cry as if I cannot stop and my husband cry too, but sometime later he tell me he going to work in the grounds and to ask the neighbour where we must bury the baby. I run over by the neighbour and she run back with me.

After she see the baby she tell me to go by the priest and ask him about burial. I wrap the baby in some cloth I have there and the neighbour lend me a dress she have for going to church. I get the bus into St. John's and I pray that nobody notice that my baby is dead. When we get to St. John's I walk, holding my baby, from the Bus-Stop to the house behind the Church where I know the priest stay. When I get there and the priest come out to see me I tell him my baby is dead and I have no money to bury him.

He look at my baby and he tell me I must go to the Free Burial Place but it is on the other side of St. John's and he give me directions which I cannot understand because I do not know the name of all the streets.

To this day I do not know how I get there, but I get there and they take my baby. A man ask me how my baby die and I tell him I do not know; last night my baby was alive and this morning I find him dead.

I never see my baby again. I stay there a while until the man come and tell me I could go now—they will bury my baby.

When I get back to the Bus Stop it was dark already and no bus was there. I so tired I lie on the bench and fall asleep. It was the next morning I did get a bus to go back to Bolans. My husband was glad to see me and when I was telling he what happen with the baby the neighbour came over and tell me she want she dress back.

Since then I did get a seersucker dress to keep for Church, Wedding, Funeral, things so. I get myself the seersucker dress one Saturday after Market when we make $6.00. I buy it for $5.00 and we go home with $1.00, but now I have my own good dress.

My second baby die too and this time I carry the baby straight to the Free Burial Place. Well I sad for a long time after. I feel that all my baby go die. One day I hear there is a Health Clinic in Jennings and the nurse there is very good, so I go to see the nurse and tell her what happen to my two children. She tell me off.

She say the next time I get pregnant I must come straight to the Clinic; and I tell her that YES I am pregnant. From that day she pay close attention to me; give me tins of thing to mix with water and drink and my third baby live and the nex' five after him. She give me bottles and milk in tin to feed my babies because she say my milk is not enough. Yes, after the first two, all six live; but through the years I lose them one, one, one.

 One daughter drown at a school picnic, one son get run down by a bus, and so it go on; but yes I has one son alive; but he, he see me when he see me—but is because after my husband die and I marry Aaron. Aaron did sometimes put he in shackles to keep he quiet while I was gone away doing my cleaning work. Well—is so it does go—God does understand all things—but my son, he will never understand.

But now Miss Doris I does own two houses, yes not one, but two house you see me here. You know when I was in school they teach us to read and they would read story to us and poetry too and there was one poetry I love above all the other—it is called The Ant & The Cricket and I never forget it and if there is one thing that teach me to save it is that poetry. So when I was a vendor and I made some money I would always save a little here and a little there no matter how small the amount is and the time come when I was in my 66th year that I buy a two room house in Golden Grove which is nearer to the market and they allow us to grow our produce on a piece of land behind the house; and then the time come when I could buy a one room house where we keep our provisions. The house near to the market; and then the day come when the Government give me a job as a cleaner and I sell the one-room house and I buy this house you see here.

"Miss Amelia I must congratulate you. You must be proud of what you have achieved."

"In truth Miss Doris, I am proud; but now I am getting old and I am not sure to who I will leave it when the time come—when I gone and Aaron too. My son, he say he don't want it. I think I will leave it to Mrs. Tonge, Gwendolyn Tonge. She good to me you hear. When I was sick, flat in the bed with a stomach pain is Mrs. Tonge who did turn me and change me and bring me a bag of the pads to wear. One day when she turning me she say 'Amelia how come you so fat? Turning you will be the end of me!' I like Mrs. Tonge too bad."

"You know Miss Amelia you tell me about that poem that mean so much to you. I would really like to hear it." Miss Doris I have it here with me and another one too. My two favourite poetry."

Amelia got up and went to a cupboard on the other side of the room. She opened the cupboard and took out a small wooden box and returned to Doris and Samantha. She put the box gently on the table and opened it. Inside were two pieces of paper yellowed with age and folded neatly. Amelia took out the first one and opened it lovingly. "This one is *The Ant & The Cricket*. Because I recite it so well my teacher type it out for me. She said I was the best in the class."

The Ant & The Cricket

A silly young cricket
Accustomed to sing
Through the warm sunny months
Of gay summer and spring,
Began to complain
When he found that his home
And his cupboard were empty
And winter had come.

Not a crumb could be found
On the snow covered ground.
Not a flower could be seen
Not a leaf on a tree.
"Oh, what will become"
Said the cricket
"Of me?"

At last, his starvation
And famine made bold,
All dripping with sweat
And all trembling with cold;
Away he set off to a miserly ant
To see if to keep him alive
He would grant.

A shelter from rain
A mouthful of grain,
He wished only to borrow

Would repay it tomorrow;
"If not I will die
Of starvation and sorrow."

Said the ant to the cricket
"I am your servant and friend,
But we ants never borrow
Nor we ants never lend.
But tell me dear sir
Did you nothing lay by
When the weather was warm?"

"Oh, not I," said the cricket
"My heart was so light
That I danced every day
And I danced every night,
For that is my nature
To dance and be gay."

"So you dance and be gay?"
Said the ant
"So you see sir, what you say?
Go then and dance all the winter away!"
Just then he hastily lifted the wicket
And out of the door
Turned the poor little cricket.

Though this is a fable
The lesson is good -
If you live without work
You will go without food.

Poet unknown

And you see this other poetry I have here — this is one my mother teach us when we were young. I recite it to my teacher and she type it out for me as well. My mother would say it over and over when we children quarrel or fight and while she saying it she would slap we with the back of she hand —

"Whatever brawl disturb the street there should be *peace* at home" buff...bap.

"Where sisters dwell and brothers meet quarrel should never come" shove, bop, slap, bang...

Well I know it by heart and I teach it to my children too —

Whatever Brawl Disturb The Street

Whatever brawl disturb the street,
There should be peace at home.
Where sisters dwell and brothers meet
Quarrels should never come.

Birds in their little nest agree
And 'tis a shameful sight
When children of one family
Fall out and fight.

Hard names at first and threatening words
That are but noisy breath,
May grow to clubs and make it swords
To murder and to death.

The devil tempt one mother's son
To rage against the other
And wicked Cain had hurried on
'Till he had killed his brother.

The wise will let the anger cool
At least before it's night
But in the bosom of a fool
It burns 'till morning light.

Are these thy favours day by day
To ME above?

The rest, then let me
Love THEE more than they
And try to love THEE best.

Pardon O LORD our childish rage
Our little brawls remove
And as we grow to riper age
Our hearts will all be loved.

Poet unknown

73

"I love that poem Miss Amelia. I must write that one down, but my pen is not in my bag. I know what we must do. We is two ladies together and we must have tea together tomorrow at four o'clock in the afternoon."

"I mus' be there Miss Doris. Ent that is what these high up women and them does do? Ent they does always have tea in the afternoon? Well, now I has two house of my own it is the right thing to do. I has some good bush tea right here in my yard. It minty, minty. I go bring some with me; but Miss Doris don't invite Aaron you hear; he have no manner and he go embarras me. I go leave some tea for he here."

So with kisses and waves Doris and Samantha left for home, and here in our ever changing lives the hand of comfort had reached across.

"Yet I will not forget you. See I have inscribed you on the palms of My hands."

Isaiah 49:15-16.

Fishing at Fort James in 1944

Fort James Pier, 1940s

I was five years old and we were on holiday in Antigua, the home of my Dad's parents, grandparents and great-grandparents. We lived in Trinidad but Dad often took his wife and children to Antigua on holiday to see our grandparents and be shown all the places Dad loved as a child.

Grandpa Willie McDonald and Grandma Hilda (who had been an Edwards) lived in a house on Redcliff Street where Grandpa practiced as a doctor; he had his Pharmacy in Friendly Alley.

On this holiday Dad had rented a lovely bungalow named Edgewater on the sea at Hodges Bay from Mr. Anjo, as there was not enough room in the house at Redcliff Street for all of us—Mum and Dad, my big brother Ian eleven years old, my big sister Heather nine years old, me aged five and Robin my baby sister aged one and a half. We all loved Antigua.

One afternoon Dad and Ian decided to go fishing at Fort James. Mum didn't want to go and neither did Heather and Robin was too young but five year old Gillie begged them to take her with them. Ian was not too keen but Dad gave in and told me I could come. I was elated. We set out for Fort James with all the fishing gear in the boot of the car and on the way there I was given instructions by my big brother that I must be quiet and not chatter because fishing was a serious business. I assured him I would be very quiet. I knew Fort James well as Dad had often brought his whole family there for a drive and I loved it. That old stone fort looking out to sea with its cannons in the ramparts of its walls. Dad said it was there to protect Antigua from pirates. I loved the Fort and I loved the long wooden jetty which stretched into the sea; this lovely jetty opened at the end into a much larger space where there was a wooden bench on either end and the men usually stood in the middle at the edge of the jetty if they were fishing. To get to the jetty you had to climb down steep concrete steps with a wooden handrail all the way down. These steps were built into the side of the cliff overlooking the harbour.

When we got to the end of the jetty Dad and Ian got their fishing equipment ready and I went over and sat on one of the benches. Such a lovely place to be looking out across the aquamarine Antiguan sea to St. John's Harbour while the sea murmured all around you and underneath you as well. Dad had shown me The Sleeping Indian, a series of mountains across the bay that looked exactly like that—A Sleeping Indian. There he was with his headdress stretching out behind him, his hooked nose, his arms folded across his chest, lying in a straight line, his upturned feet at the end. He had been lying there since God made Antigua and would keep guard over us for many centuries to come. I sat there looking across at him and also seeing all the boats coming into harbor for the evening. I loved the little tugs best of all. There was something so warm, strong and safe about the way they looked as they came chugging in. Sometimes I would see a Captain at the wheel with his Captain's cap on. Sometimes they were pulling along barges full of heavy items much bigger than the small tug itself. I dreamed that one day I would be the captain of a tug. It was lovely sitting there dreaming with the protection of The Sleeping Indian in front of me and the cannons of Fort James behind me and my Dad and brother throwing their lines into the sea.

Fort James with view of Sleeping Indian, 1940s

Heather, Mum, Robin, Gillian, Dad and Grandma Hilda
McDonald in background - Edgewater 1944.

Edgewater in 1944.

But then....my Dad out of the goodness of his soul, made a suggestion that was to spoil the rest of the afternoon for all of us.

Dad had been worrying about me sitting all by myself on the bench and decided to call me over—"Gillie come and sit next to us. You can count the fish and keep an eye on them." Dad and Ian had caught five fish and they were on the jetty next to Dad. I went over and sat on the jetty near to the fish but I didn't really want to look at them, when suddenly the little fish nearest the end of the jetty gave a leap and flipped over the edge. I was about to tell Dad what had happened but as I gazed over into the water I saw the fish right itself and then a moment later it swam away like lightning. A feeling of joy went through me and I made the instant decision to push all the fish back in. Something told me not to tell Dad and Ian....so I sat there innocently gazing out to sea, my right hand holding on to the edge of the jetty while my left hand slowly edged the four remaining fish to the edge and then one by one over they went! I looked over and saw one righting itself and then swimming away but I didn't have time to look for the others because just at this moment Dad looked down and exclaimed, "Where are all the fish??!" I felt as shocked as Dad but for a different reason.....I suddenly realized that

I would have to give an explanation about what had happened to the fish to Dad and Ian—"They...they...fell over the side," I said. "They FELL over?!" Dad said in disbelief. I started to explain what had happened to the first fish, how it had flipped over the side but decided to include ALL the fish in the flip..... "they all gave a big flip, fell over the side and then they swam away. You see Dad they were all ALIVE," but neither Dad or Ian believed me. My brother said, "I don't believe a word she says. You will never come fishing with us again!" Dad said nothing. I went back and sat on the bench and Dad and Ian resumed fishing; but they never caught anything else and after about twenty minutes they packed up their gear and we headed back to the car. Nobody talked to me on the way home. I thought Mum and Heather would understand, but Mum said— "You should never have pushed the fish back in after Dad and Ian were kind enough to take you with them" and Heather said "Why did you do such a thing?! Now they'll never take you fishing again," and me? Well I was left with a secret feeling of joy at seeing the fish swim away not believing their good luck.

I was five years old then and today seventy years later when I go to Fort James that memory remains very clear in my mind; but today the lovely jetty with its benches and even the concrete steps leading down to it with a handrail all the way down—all of this is gone, washed away by the sea and various storms, never to be re-built; so there's nowhere one can stand and fish.

The Sleeping Indian lies there with his arms folded over his chest protecting Antigua; and Fort James with its cannons in the ramparts of its walls protects Antigua from the other side. And to this day I have a special love for Tug Boats whenever I see one passing by.

Painted by Gillian years after the 'Fishing at Fort James' story when
Gillian was married and had children of her own. The lovely old jetty was
no longer usable, destroyed over the years by weather and neglect; but
The Sleeping Indian still lies there protecting us all.

Mrs. Jarvis and the Devil

Hodges Bay Mansion is a beautiful old house built of stone on the Caribbean island of Antigua. Built in the 16th century on 3 acres of land, on the sea, with its own beach. It is a low lying and sprawling mansion, its main quarters made up of the living room, dining room, music parlour, facing east onto a lovely stone verandah which overlooked a croquet lawn. The verandah always looked cool and inviting with potted palms and ferns, comfortable armchairs with small wooden tables beside them to place ones drink and/or snack. The four cool and spacious bedrooms faced north-east overlooking the startling shades of blue of the sea around a coral island, which Antigua is. The dining room or Battery as it was called was a long stone wing on the western side of the house with doors to the stone kitchen at the far end. It is said to be the oldest house in Antigua, built in 1694.

The three acres of land on which it stands are beautifully landscaped with lawns and red and yellow flamboyant trees planted in each corner, their umbrella-like branches shading the lawn and giving bursts of colour to the already beautiful picture when they are in flower in the months of June, July and August.

In the middle of the front stone patio is a huge mahogany tree which shades the entire patio and gives a sense of coolness, even in the middle of the hottest day with the sun filtering through its leaves and making patterns on the stones. It was also famous for the giant cactus growing beside the wall of the battery. Once a year this cactus flowered with an extraordinary flower people named 'the moon flower' because it was completely round in shape and a luminous white that seemed to shine at night with its own light and

Moon Cactus

was the size of two mature hands spread wide.

These flowers would always open on the night of the full moon, usually in August. Sometimes there was only one but as many as six had been known to have opened at one time. They only stayed open for two days and nights. The flowers did not seem to leave a seed and nobody had ever been able to grow it by piece. Hodges Bay House is carved on the ancient stone gateposts at the entrance.

This beautiful house changed hands over the years as its different owners died or went back to Britain and in the 20th century it became the home of Dalmer and Maybert Dew. Dalmer was the son of the owner and manager of Dew & Company. He had arrived from England as a young boy with his father and mother. His father had proceeded to build up a flourishing merchant business but was now retired and Dalmer had taken his place as Manager of Dew and Company.

His wife Maybert descended from an old Antiguan family named Jarvis who had come over from Britain over a century ago. Maybert was also an only child. Maybert and Dalmer had lived at first in the capital of Antigua, St. John's.

Dalmer was very happy living in the town. He would walk to work in the morning, moving at a brisk pace in the fresh early morning air, whistling to himself as he walked down the hilly roads of St. John's until he reached Dew and Company on the waterfront. He loved his early morning walk when the air was still cool, the Laughing Gulls were calling to each other as they flew overhead and the bells of St. John's Cathedral were ringing for seven o'clock service. It always gave him a feeling of a new beginning; he walked

Maybert and Dalmer's house. Photo by Skene Howie.

back home at noon where he and Maybert sat down to a delicious lunch, cooked for them by their beloved cook Elma, their linen napkins crisp and clean, the silver shining. Elma had been with the Dew family for years. After lunch he would lie in his long chair on their cool stone verandah shaded by wooden louvres and pots of luxuriant green ferns. He slept for an hour and would return to work for 2 p.m., refreshed.

Dew and Company closed on the dot of four o'clock, as did every other business in Antigua; Dalmer would return home for tea with a hot muffin or Jacobs Cream Crackers with butter and guava jam—his favourite; then he would shower, change into fresh clothes and around five thirty would walk over to The New Club which was 'For Men Only' where he enjoyed the comraderie of friends and fellow business acquaintances, games of Bridge and Pool and glasses of 'refreshment.' He would always be home by eight o'clock for dinner.

Maybert kept herself busy with her Womens Church Association of which her mother, Mrs. Jarvis, was the President and Maybert the Vice-President. They visited the sick at the hospital, the Old Peoples Home and The Mental Institution among others. They arranged tea parties and coffee mornings where the ladies gossiped about the island and its comings and goings while they knitted little things like socks, shawls and vests for the inmates of the institutions they visited.

On Sundays there was Service at nine a.m. at the Cathedral on the hill overlooking the Capital and afterwards they often went to Fort James for a swim and a picnic lunch.

Then one day the owner of Hodges Bay House died, his wife went to live with their daughter in Britain and Hodges Bay House was put up for sale. Maybert was overjoyed and set her heart on making Hodges Bay House her home. She had been to many dinners and parties there, at first as a young girl with her parents and in more recent years with Dalmer.

On the other hand Dalmer was reticent to move from their comfortable home in town and at first would not agree; however in the end, Maybert, with the help of her mother Mrs. Jarvis, persuaded Dalmer to buy the Hodges Bay House and they moved in.

Dalmer liked the lovely grounds and the beauty of the old stone house itself and it was nice to be able to step outside onto his own coral white beach and have a swim whenever he felt like it; but without quite knowing how to explain it, even to himself, he suddenly felt a loneliness he'd never felt before. He missed walking to work in the early mornings; now he'd had to get a car and although he knew how to drive, was a very nervous driver, so he had hired a chauffeur, Mr. Bridgewater. Mr. Bridgewater was given a special uniform with cap to match and was taught to bow when opening the door for ladies—which all went perfectly with their new home—but somehow it was never the same.....never the same as walking briskly to work in the early morning, whistling to himself, with all the accompanying sounds, smells and sights of St. John's at that hour.

Also his evenings at The New Club became less and less as he could no longer walk there and the car was in use most afternoons for Maybert to visit her mother or different friends and much of the time Maybert wanted her husband to visit with her; when they were not visiting Maybert was having parties of her own which needed the presence of himself.....and worse was yet to come for Dalmer.

About two years after they'd moved into Hodges Bay House Maybert's father died and her mother, Mrs. Jarvis, came to live with them.

Mrs. Jarvis was a dogmatic, bullying old lady, who tried to rule everyones lives; she even bullied Maybert which is saying a lot, as Maybert herself had inherited her mothers domineering personality.

Mrs. Jarvis took over the running of Hodges Bay House and was forever telling Dalmer what he could or could not do and Dalmer, being of a quiet, reticent, nervous nature, never put his foot down, which he was certainly entitled to do, as it was his money that bought the Hodges Bay House. Instead, by giving in all the time, he added fuel to Mrs. Jarvis' already domineering nature.

Dalmer found refuge in his work as Manager of Dew and company and was 'allowed' to come home late twice a week (seven o'clock—dinner-time). On these two evenings Dalmer would leave work at four o'clock and walk up to The New Club and these days at his club were the times he looked forward to most. His chauffeur would meet him at 6.30 and drive him home in time for dinner.

Maybert was too busy to notice as she arranged her dinners, croquet parties on the front lawn, tea parties, coffee mornings and helped her mother make up guests lists. Their dinner parties were held in The Battery, adjoining the Living Room. Originally the kitchen, it was built entirely of stone with very thick walls and at its western end was a big fireplace. Above the fireplace hung an ancient sword, now polished and shining, that Dalmer had found as a young boy on one of his excursions in the hills. Every year there was a Christmas Party and a fire was always lit in the fireplace for that occasion. It was one of the few occasions Dalmer enjoyed, as, dressed in his Evening Suit he proposed toast upon toast.....to King George VI and the Queen Mother, the Administrator, the Chief Minister, friends romans, countrymen and so on.....the wine was poured as the toasts continued and afterwards everyone danced and sang as the band played.

A few years passed in this way until Mrs. Jarvis reached the age of eighty when she became very ill and was put to bed. Doctor Winter visited every day, did what he could, but every day she became weaker. Eventually she lapsed into a state of unconsciousness. Doctor Winter advised the family that Mrs. Jarvis was dying and it was now only a question of a few days.

During the time of her illness Dalmer had become stronger, more manly; he'd actually taken charge of some of the family affairs so that Maybert could be with her mother and had even begun visiting on his own to tell friends and family how Mrs. Jarvis was.

When Doctor Winter advised himself and Maybert that it was now only a question of days he told his wife not to worry about anything; he would take charge of everything. Dalmer, with his face fixed in a mournful expression, left the house with his chauffeur to visit friends and family members; he explained the situation in subdued terms and asked if he, he and he would be bearers at the funeral when the sad event occurred, which, sadly to say, would be very soon. He made all the arrangements at the Funeral Home and ordered a beautiful, expensive coffin, all padded inside with blue velvet.

Everyone at Hodges Bay House walked softly and sadly as befitted the occasion.

It was sunset and, standing at the door looking onto the patio, Dalmer noticed that their priceless cactus was flowering; one of its moon flowers was already open and seemed to shine in the dusk; as he was looking at this a commotion suddenly broke out in the courtyard; a fight was taking place between the two family dogs and one had the other by the throat..Dalmer ran into The Battery, grabbed his ancient sword from above the fireplace and ran towards the dogs brandishing his sword and shouting; the dogs ran off in different directions, one of them colliding with Maisie, a black goat whom Dalmer had adopted about a month previously when it had strayed onto their property as a tiny kid. Maisie panicked, ran into the house through the open front door, ran through the living room, through the half opened door of Mrs. Jarvis' bedroom and tried to jump over the bed but instead landed on top of Mrs. Jarvis for a second before jumping off the other side and out of the window.

To everyones amazement Mrs. Jarvis raised her head from her pillow, her arms in the air and her eyes wide open, screaming, *'Save me! Save me! The Devil has come for me!'*

Mrs. Jarvis recovered and lived on for another twelve years!!

Shortly afterwards Dalmer had a nervous breakdown and Maybert was advised by Doctor Winter to take him to England for some 'cool autumn air', which she did, but he was never the same again.

"The best laid schemes o' mice an' men / Gang aft a-gley..."

Robert Burns

Margetson Ward

Holberton Hospital, Antigua
14th–21st May, 2002

Margetson Ward is a long, low building on a rise and facing east. It is part of the Main Building and Casualty Ward. It is cool as there are windows all along the eastern wall open to the constant easterly Trade Winds and it is in the shade of three huge Samaan trees with their umbrella-like branches stretching out over all the nearby buildings. My bed-head is against the eastern wall, under a window, and next to the Staff Desk. Alongside of me are five other beds against the eastern wall and at the end of the ward is the bathroom. There is a passage way in the middle with a wide table in the centre on which all the food is served, the basins for the early morning wash filled, etc. and then against the opposite wall are 6 more beds, facing east—twelve in all.

There is a railing around the top of each bed with curtains that are pulled whenever one uses the bed-pan or has a sponge-off. Sheets are changed every other day, but sometimes there are not enough sheets and then the nurses have to choose which beds need changing the most. The nurses shifts are 7 to 3, 3 to 11 and 11 to 7 (the graveyard shift). The nurses always arrive in fresh, starched uniforms and caps and nurses watches on little chains pinned to their blouses. They seem very efficient and there is a Head Nurse (Sister) in charge of each shift.

Patients temperature, pulse and blood pressure are taken three times a day and there is a file on how each patient is doing at the bottom of each bed. These files are all placed on the Staff Desk at the beginning of the 7 a.m. shift for the Sister in charge to check over and show to the different doctors when they arrive to see their own patients. Some of the nurses are Cubans. Early each morning

Holberton Hospital 1950s -
Margetson Ward is just opposite to the nurse.

the whole ward is mopped with disinfectant and a strong young man with the muscles of a wrestler and a hairstyle of little black plaits sticking out all over his head like a hedgehog strolls jauntily through the ward up to the bathroom, a toilet pump swinging in his hand like a baton. Then he strolls back through the ward in the same fashion the toilet having been cleaned for the day. Sometimes they have to call him in at other times.

There is a nice lady in the bed next to me—Mrs. Violet Allen. Mrs. Allen must be in her 60's and is very thin. Her face with its high cheekbones and wide apart eyes must have been quite beautiful once but is now very drawn. The nurses keep trying to get her to eat more and they bring special food for her from the kitchen. Her daughter Joslyn comes every morning at 7 with a special breakfast for her Mum and to take away her used nightie and put a fresh one in her bedside table. I notice that everyone in the ward always has on a fresh, pretty nightie every morning after the sponge-off. Some of Mrs. Allen's family usually visit again between 10 and 12 and 5 and 7; her husband Alfred comes every night between 7 and 9. He always brings a flask of tea for Mrs. Allen with him and a small battery radio and sits beside her; sometimes they talk; sometimes she sleeps and he listens to his radio while smoothing down her bed with his hands. He is an old man, thin and upright in posture; he wears a straw hat and has a kind face with lines of character put in over the years, like his wife. She tells me they live in Green Bay (poorest area in Antigua); she was born in Green Bay Violet Lindsey and married Alfred Allen also of Green Bay when she was 19. They have 5 children. She tells me that the 96 year old lady in the bed at the very end of the ward who has just had the operation on her hip to have a new hip-ball and pin put in (the same I was supposed to have) was her mid-wife for her first three babies; the other two were born in the hospital. She tells me 10 of them live in their small house in Green Bay—Herself, Alfred, Joslyn and her 4 children and one of her sons and his 2 children. Alfred has a job with the Workers Union.

Mrs. Allen has a gentle, refined voice. I like her very much. I wonder what she is in hospital for. She sits up in bed and washes herself in the morning; she uses her bedpan by herself which the nurses leave on a chair beside her bed. She is far more independent that way than I am who is not yet allowed to sit up on my own and cannot turn on my fractured left side to pick up my bedpan on my own. Whatever she has it cannot be as bad as me, I think.

Two days after meeting her I ask why she is in hospital and she pulls down the sheet and shows me that her leg has been cut off just below the knee—I am horrified—"Oh Dear God" I think to myself, "and I think I am badly done by." She tells me she broke her toe two months ago and it would not heal and gangrene set in mainly due to the fact that she has diabetes. At first the doctors cut off her toe, then all her toes, then her foot, and now her leg under the knee. Now they think at last it has begun to heal and she thanks God. She tells me it is the first time in a while that she is almost without pain. She keeps her Bible next to her and often when I look across during the day she is reading it. Her minister from the Moravian Church visits her quite often and prays with her, telling her that God is with her through all her trials and will be with her always. She has been in the hospital for 6 weeks.

The day before I left her stitches were removed and the doctors told her she would be going home this week. I am so glad for her.

In the bed next to Mrs. Allen is Mrs. Barnes, an elderly lady, who can get out of bed and walk to the bathroom by herself and walk into the nurse's office to make herself a cup of tea. She is well on the mend from whatever brought her in and will be leaving in a couple of days. She is a real chatterbox and talks to Mrs. Allen constantly. Mrs. Allen often falls asleep while she is talking to her. Mrs. Barnes is always speaking about her pets—her 3 cats, her 2 dogs, her 2 roosters and 3 hens. She talks of her cats especially, how they come up to her to tell her what they want and she gets it for them; how she buys special food at Epicurean for them; how her roosters are the best looking roosters in the whole street and can crow the loudest; how her dogs protect her; but it is the cats who talk to her and keep her company. The talk about pets started because of a cat miaowing loudly just outside of our ward. The nurses were asked about her and they said she was crying for her 4 kittens whom different nurses had taken home as pets now that they were weaned. The mother lives outside the ward and is fed by the nurses. On my first night in Margetson Ward when I was desperate for a bedpan and there were no nurses around Mrs. Barnes went into the adjoining ward to call one for me.

In the bed opposite to me is a very old lady whom the nurses call 'Miss Lucy.' Miss Lucy has big rolling eyes, no teeth, and has reached senility. She is very lovable. She's returned to infancy and has the look of a 2 year old once more. She spends most of the day making and re-making her bed. I tell her 'good morning' every morning and she raises her hand and mumbles and murmurs something that must mean good morning in return. I never did find out what was wrong with Miss Lucy except that because of her senility and the fact that she lived by herself she had been admitted to the Mental Hospital and they had sent her to Holberton Hospital when she became ill. The good news is that before I left I was told by the nurses that Miss Lucy's niece (who came to see her every evening) was going to take Miss Lucy home to live with her.

Another inmate of the Mental Hospital was in Margetson Ward—a very attractive young girl who looked about 16 years old. She was a bed down from Miss Lucy. She is fair skinned with short, black curly hair and huge black eyes. She spends most of her time sitting cross-legged in the middle of her bed with a vacant, worried look on her face. Sometimes she gets up and runs to the toilet at the top of the ward and sometimes she runs down to the Nurses Desk to show them something on her leg or her arm but she doesn't say anything. Otherwise she is lying down with the sheet pulled up to her neck. Visiting hours are 10–12, 3–5, 7–9, but she never has any visitors. Sometimes she sits cross-legged on her bed looking at everyone else's visitors and sometimes she just pulls her sheet over her head.

I never hear her speaking and I wish that I could go over and speak to her.

I asked Mrs. Allen about her. Mrs. Allen tells me she has been in the ward for 5 weeks. She tells me that she is a retarded girl who was viciously raped and became more demented afterwards. Her family had then had her admitted to the Mental Home (known in Antigua as 'the madhouse'). While in the Mental Home she'd become ill and they had her admitted to the Hospital where she was given a bed in Margetson Ward and attended to. When she was better the Mental Home sent attendants to take her back with them but she screamed and held on to the bed and cried that her father was coming for her. The nurses got together and told the Mental Home that she was not well enough yet to return and since then they'd been making up different stories to try and keep her from being re-admitted. Her father had never visited during the 5 weeks she'd been in Margetson.

That poor girl. I feel so sorry for her. I wonder what she must think as she sits there on her bed and sees all the different people coming and going and nobody paying her the slightest attention. I think she feels she does not belong anywhere, unwanted and unloved; but maybe the nurses have at least given her a feeling of safety.

One night when I couldn't sleep and lay there on my back trying to get as comfortable as I could I looked around the ward (the nurses had forgotten to put out the overhead lights) and everyone seemed to be sleeping except for this young, gentle looking girl who was sitting cross-legged on her bed looking around the ward with her enormous black eyes. I waved to her but she didn't seem to notice; there were no nurses in the ward and everything was very quiet. I closed my eyes and tried to sleep only to open them a short time later to see this young girl standing right beside my bed, looking down at me. I smiled and put out my hand and asked her name and she put her hand out stiffly in a sort of robot motion and said in a soft, childlike voice, 'my name is Dorothy.' I told Dorothy that I wanted to come and speak to her but I couldn't leave my bed because I'd broken my hip, so she must come and speak to me sometimes. She didn't answer but said instead, 'I hope you sleep well' and then returned to her bed and pulled the sheet over her head. She never did come back to see me but I felt the only time she'd had the courage to visit me was when the ward was as quiet as it was that night. Two days before I left a lady about 40ish came to see Dorothy with a gift. The gift was an attractive 'pants-suit' which Dorothy was very excited about and the nurses pulled the curtains around her bed and helped her to put it on. When they pulled the curtains back there she was in her new suit, looking so pretty. Then she jumped into bed and pulled the sheet up to her neck.

About an hour later the same lady returned; put Dorothy's few things into a bag and left with Dorothy. The nurses told me the lady is her aunt and has taken Dorothy to live with her. I pray that Dorothy will be in a place where she feels secure and loved.

On my 2nd day in Margetson a large lady (huge, must have been about 6 feet) was wheeled in from the operating theatre and put on the bed to the right of Miss Lucy. This 'lady' was something else— when she recovered consciousness she wouldn't let the nurses near her. She shouted obscenities and threw her pillows at them and then rolled her covering sheet into a ball and threw that as well.

She had on a 'Depend' and they wanted to change her and told her, 'Eh, Eh, what wrong with you? You want to stay there with your stinky poo poo'? and she shouted back, 'Is my own poo poo and you all can't touch it! You all more stinky than me.....you look like mud people'! When her family came later on to visit they changed and washed her and put on a fresh nightie and all was quiet behind the curtains. She was truly one of the ugliest old ladies I've seen— very black, her face wrinkled and warlike, bushy grey eyebrows over small sunken eyes, no teeth, a hooked nose and pointed chin; her hair was uncombed and sticking out all over the place and she had a little white moustache and beard. She looked strong and muscular. She only stayed for 2 days. She was just as difficult with the nurses on the 2nd day and they were relieved when her doctor said she could go home. Her daughter-in-law and her husband came for her. Her daughter-in-law was a nice looking young girl and looked small compared with her mother-in-law! Her husband was also smaller than her; a nice looking elderly man, slim, with a walking stick and cap. He apologised to the nurses on behalf of his wife. He said, 'This woman give me trouble from the Day One. Like she have no manners.' The daughter-in-law pulled the curtains and helped her to dress, the husband giving her long lectures all the while and not a peep from her. When they wheeled her out in a chair she smiled for the first time but said nothing when her husband told her to say goodbye to the nurses and apologise.

The morning after 'Mrs. Difficult' left a new patient was wheeled in from the operating room for that bed. Both her feet were heavily bandaged but as they wheeled her past my bed I saw that the bandages were soaked in blood and it was dripping onto the floor, forming two pools of blood when the stretcher stopped by her bed. The nurses got mops and buckets and rolls of fresh bandage and pulled the curtains around the bed. When the curtains were pulled back the lady was in bed on a Drip and her bandages looked clean. Her name is Mrs. Bruce and she has leprosy.....poor thing! I didn't realise that leprosy still existed in Antigua. It seems you can get it through inherited genes or sex with someone who has it. She had also lost most of her fingers.

Her family came and went looking sad and worried bringing her flowers, fresh nighties, delicacies and love. One lady in particular was with her every morning and evening and often washed and dressed her if the nurses were busy. Mrs. Bruce has a very nice face;

we would wave and tell each other good morning in the mornings and when I was trying to walk on the crutches with Dougs help she would offer words of encouragement and so would my friend Mrs. Allen. The morning of the day I left (21st May) I was sad to hear her doctor telling her that there would have to be further surgery. She looked so worried and her family looked sad and worried when they came. Yet she still smiled and waved to me as I was leaving and hoped my hip would soon be healed. By this time I was beginning to think of my injury as a minor thing.

One night, it must have been about one in the morning, when I could not sleep but was lying comfortably in bed with my eyes closed; the overhead lights were off and all was quiet in the ward; I could hear the murmur of the nurses in the 'tea room' adjoining the ward and suddenly I heard a lovely young voice burst into song—a beautiful old irish melody, 'The Mountains of Morne.'

I felt the tears running down my face, thinking to myself how extraordinary life is—here I am in a public ward in Holberton Hospital with a broken hip listening to a young antiguan nurse singing 'The Mountains of Morne' at one o'clock in the morning...... Life! the beauty of it.....the sadness of it.....the happiness.....the grief.

I lay there remembering our playroom in St.Augustine when I was growing up, with our gramophone and the big cupboard full of old 78's which had once belonged to Grandma and Grandpa McDonald. They loved music and used to have musical evenings at their home once a month. One side of the cupboard was filled with Irish, Scottish and English songs sung by famous singers of their time, the other side was filled with classicals and operas. I remember we had some by the famous Caruso. I used to love listening to the Irish, Scottish and English folk songs and would play them over and over again getting to know many of them by heart. 'The 'Mountains of Morne' was one of them...

I had been there about 5 days when a lady was brought in from the operating room and put in a bed at the top of the ward.

Towards evening she started crying out for the nurses who would come and adjust her position and the different gadgets she was attached to; I didn't sleep very well that night as this poor lady seemed to be calling out to the nurses and God for help all night. I started calling for a nurse to come and help her as well. A nurse came and re-assured me that she was okay but wanted to be turned and she (the nurse) was waiting on someone to help her turn the patient. Not an easy job by herself as the patient is attached to a drip and a catheter.

The next morning Mrs. Allen told me that this patient has had both eyes removed. I say, 'but WHY? WHY?' and Mrs. Allen told me it's because she'd been having terrible headaches. I couldn't believe that was the only reason and my night-nurse Leonora found out from the nurses that this poor woman had already lost the sight in both her eyes and was suffering from unbearable headaches that no pill could ease. Something like cancerous growths behind the eyes. I am learning how to pray for other people instead of myself.

On Sunday morning two ladies from St. Georges Church (where Mum & Dad and Grandpa McDonald are buried) came in to give our ward a beautiful bouquet of flowers from their Pentecostal Service. They placed it on the food table on the corner closest to me, and facing me—a bouquet of red roses, white chrysanthemums and yellow gladioli mixed with fern. I think to myself, 'They are from Mum and Dad.'

It is a lovely time of the morning—7 a.m.—everyone has washed and are in their fresh nighties, the nurses have opened the windows and tied the curtains; the fresh breeze is blowing through the ward and our beds are covered in sunshine. The ward is very quiet. Some patients are asleep and some, like my friend Mrs. Allen beside me, are reading their Bibles. I also have my favourite Bible beside me, (Cathy's Bible from Achtercairn School in Gairloch). The lady who had been crying all night is asleep.

Later on Sunday morning, two women—ex prostitutes who had at one time tried to commit suicide and are now born again Christians—came to sing hymns to everyone in the ward. Many of the patients joined in the singing and I tried also but only knew the words of one of the hymns. The two ladies were a bit nervous and one had a lovely voice.

A short time after a group of one young man, one old man and two old women came to give a short sermon on God's Love and gave everyone a blessing. They also sang two hymns. They were from the Pentecostal Church.

I didn't sleep soundly for any long periods while I was in the hospital and it was on the Sunday night around midnight I heard the Main door being opened and some voices speaking softly. I opened my eyes and saw the nurses bringing in a very attractive young woman dressed in party finery and her hair long and beautifully plaited with sequins and beads;they helped her into the empty bed next to Mrs. Allen and pulled the sheet up for her. They did not wake her up at 4.30 with the rest of us but let her sleep until breakfast came in at nine. I was told that she had attempted suicide after a quarrel with her boyfriend, by drinking bleach. Luckily she had been rushed to hospital in time and her stomach pumped out. Her sister and a friend came for her later on that morning. I hope she will never consider such a thing again.

I left in the wheelchair with Doug on the Tuesday afternoon exactly one week after my fall.

I had my cry the day after I returned home while I was telling Cynthia about Mrs. Allen losing her leg and suddenly I started to cry and then I cried for everyone in Margetson Ward.

Oh Dear God I am so thankful for all the blessings You have given me.

Thank you for the love, security and care of my beloved husband Doug whom I love so much, my beloved children Cathy and Skene and their love and for all my brothers, sisters, family and friends who sent me their messages of love. I am so lucky.

I can only pray that my friends in Margetson Ward will feel the peace of Your love and that all their ailments will be healed and that Dorothy will find the security and love she needs with her aunt.

I can and will never forget my week in Margetson Ward.

The Clinic

The Catholic church in Antigua had just built a small wooden house in one of the poorer areas and was using it as a Clinic for the surrounding residents.

Miss Julie, one of the parishioners, was asked if she could run the clinic every Tuesday afternoon between two and four. Miss Julie agreed and was given a short course on how to take blood pressure, test for sugar, take temperatures and a few other simple things.

The small, wooden house was on an open plot of land with one coconut tree. It was placed on twelve flat stones, three under each corner of the house. There were two reasons for this—the first reason being the land had been loaned to the church by the owner with the agreement that if the owner needed the land in the future the wooden house would be removed; if this happened the house could then be lifted onto the back of a trailer and taken to some other location; the second reason was that it would be elevated in case of heavy rain and flooding. As there was no running water there Miss Julie always brought with her a large plastic bottle of drinking water and clean towels for use in the Clinic. Inside there was a table which held a plastic basin, a jug, and twelve drinking glasses; then there was Miss Julie's chair and eight others. There was a large open drain between the road and the piece of land and a few pieces of flat wood had been placed across the drain to form a 'bridge' over to the Clinic. There were always some goats, chickens and a few stray dogs wandering around.

Miss Julie soon became friendly with her patients and as the weeks went by she realised that the same people came every Tuesday with occasionally a new face coming in for the first time.

Often, while waiting to be checked by Miss Julie, heated conversations would go on between the patients.....

TUESDAY January 1993

Miss Julie, "Well ladies" (no men had arrived yet), "good afternoon. Is good to see you here. Let us hope the blood pressure has not gone up again Miss Daisy. I hope you took your medication this morning before you come here to frighten me this afternoon!"

"Eh, eh, Miss Julie, don't worry your head; I feeling good today and I regular on my medication the past week since I get frighten myself last week when you tell me the pressure 180 over 120 and I must go to my doctor; *but look who coming today!* is Miss Amelia— like since you move down the next road we never see you."

"Well Miss Daisy is further to walk here now and besides, this time of the day, half past two, I like to rest my head and by the time my head come off the pillow Miss Julie done close the Clinic..... and besides too, Miss Julie, my granddaughter does take up plenty of my time these past weeks. She growing up now you know, is thirteen she be last birthday and she getting too vain for she own good. The other day when she was looking in the mirror and fixing her face for what seem like an hour, I say to she, "You spending too much time with you face; remember what your great aunt Anna say—she say,

'My face I don't mind it because I'm behind it; it's the ones in the front get the jarr.'.... and I start to laugh.

Everyone started to laugh.....

"And what your granddaughter say?"

"She say, 'a jar? a jar of what'?"

"Well I was laughing because I remember I say the same thing to aunt Anna and she tell me, 'like they don't teach the children anything in school these days. Is another word for FRIGHT,' and then she start laughing away. Is laugh I laugh now but I didn't laugh then!"

When everyone stopped laughing Miss Daisy turned to Miss Amelia saying......

."....but Miss Amelia, what you think of what happen in Parliament on Monday when I hear Hugh Maxwell get on?"

"Well, Miss Daisy, I could tell you one thing, I like the way our Prime Minister tell him off. When you hear the way our Prime Minister talk you *know* he is a man of high education. You hear when he say he cannot *condone* anything of that nature, that he cannot stand the *Vituperation* people here in Antigua sink down to? He is a man who can use these *big, big* words—and why?—because he is destined for *big* places!"

"Eh, Miss Amelia, I never hear a word like *vitupation* in my life. I sure you don't even know what it mean. You just like to sound big yourself..."

"Well, Miss Daisy, I really sorry for you and your poor education; you don't know what *vitupassion* means?"

"Why you don't tell us Miss Amelia? I waiting to hear and Miss Julie too."

"That word—Miss Daisy—*that* word is something only high people with university education use—so now you could see from where the Prime Minister come—but I know it because my teacher always tell me that I have more sense than I need.

That word mean a person who take so much vitamin that he cannot control the *passion* in his voice.....like it shout out of control.....and the Prime Minister go on to say we are all *consumed*, which means, Miss Julie, we consume too much vitamin."

"Well, Miss Amelia, the Prime Minister should not talk of medical things like vitamins, he should stick to his politics; and where you see all this thing anyway?"

"I see it in The Sentinel this week."

As this conversation was coming to an end Miss Julie noticed another patient coming through the door.....

"Here comes Miss Olive. It's good to see you. Let us see how the sugar is today; I have my testers here."

"I too glad Nurse Julie. Like I not feeling a hundred percent this week and besides I so glad to see you. Is before Christmas the last time I come here and I miss my friends I meet at the Clinic—look here come Miss Ruby..."

"Good-afternoon nurse Julie I just passing on my way home from work and I see the door open and your head by the window and I feel like my pressure up today.....but eh, eh, nurse Julie, what happen down by you? You all never going to hold your Primary, or what?"

"Look Miss Ruby, is I, Olive, could tell you something about that. St. John's rural north is my own constituency and I go to most of the meeting; and look how many people we have wanting to take the Old Man's place...I think is five. Poor Mathias I feel sorry for he; how they could make him lose his job before he enter? I could understand if he win the Primary...but the one I like is Miss Maginley. It is time a woman take charge of a constituency."

"Let me tell you Miss Olive, Miss Maginley too nice a person for that kind of thing; but all the same I like she too and you know she done a lot of good things for Antigua. I feel she is a dedicated person. You know that nice choir called The Community Players? I think she is one of the first member...I love to hear them. Remember the time they perform down by Heritage Quay and all sorts of old time thing was there? Moko Jumbie an' that. They still show it on TV from time to time; and if you read her pamphlet I like what she has in mind; my bones getting weary now and she say she will care for old people and open daycare centers for us; also she say she going to offer incentive to young people to join the Police Force. I like to hear of good young people in the Police; we need a strong Police Force to deal with all the badness nowadays.....but what of you Miss Julie? Ent is you constituency as well?"

"Well, the Lord knows who I will vote for. I only wish the Old Man would come back. I feel nobody could take his place. The Old Man is the only one who really care for the people of Antigua.. I wish I could see one of the others do what he do."

Miss Daisy piped in, "True, true. I remember after hurricane Hugo when our post with all the electricity and telephone lines fall down. Well, some time after, the government put up a new post but they forget to put a street light on it and our street was in darkness. I did write a letter to the Old Man about it and two weeks later—it was a Saturday I will never forget—I was hanging out the washing at the back of the house when my husband came running to me saying in a loud voice,

'The Prime Minister is outside by the gate and he asking for you! Like you write him a letter?!!'

The washing drop from my hand, 'May the Lord have mercy 'pon my soul'! what I could have said in my letter to have our Prime

Minister come to see me?!! I feel my knees go weak. I go with my husband to the gate.

Mr. Bird was standing there dressed in a smart suit and I think it was Mr. Edwards with him and his car and chauffeur was on the other side of the road.

Mr. Bird take off his hat and put it to his chest and smiled at us..... 'Good morning Mr. and Mrs. Carter. I received your letter Mrs. Carter and I have come to ask you where you would like your street light.'

'Thank you Mr. Bird' I say in a trembling voice, 'it use to be on the electricity pole right here by our gate but the old one fall down in hurricane Hugo and when they put the new one up they forget the light.'

'The light will be there next week Mrs. Carter,' he said to me.

'Thank you very much Prime Minister, thank you very much,' was all I could say but my eyes fill with tears that he come there himself to tell me; then he made a little bow to me, put on his hat and he and Mr. Edwards return to his car.....and really by the next week the light was back."

"Well Miss Daisy is really true. That is the way he stop you know. He really care about us. I wonder if we will ever have someone like him again?.....but look who we have here.....is Perseverance."

Perseverance lived in a small house on a piece of land three streets away and further down by the mangrove swamp. Many things lived in the mangrove; herons, oysters lived on the stems and there were lots of fish. When the tide was out everyone in that area would go with their bags to pick up the mullet which had been left behind in the mud 'hundreds of them just flapping there in the mud. Those are the nights we have fish for dinner and enough for the next day too.' Perseverance grew his own tomatoes, sweet potatoes, pumpkin and eddoes and he had three banana trees, a mango tree, an orange tree and a breadfruit tree.

Miss Julie never did know what his real name was but he was a shoemaker. He made shoes and mended shoes and everyone called him Perseverance because every week when the Clinic opened Perseverance came over to ask if anyone wanted shoes made or repaired. He had made two pairs of shoes for Miss Julie's husband and repaired many belonging to the different patients who came to the Clinic. He was an ardent cricket fan and had played for his school when he was a boy. He was always saving money to buy batteries for his radio so he could listen to the sports news. Miss Julie felt he must have had a good education because he spoke like a teacher or a minister.

A short while later Mr. Wesley was seen coming through the door. Mr. Wesley was an old man who lived in the area and sometimes took up collection in church on Sundays. He always looked well dressed and always had a pipe in his mouth and wore a mustard coloured beret with a badge on it.

Mr. Wesley said to Perseverance :

"Hello friend; I saw you going into the Clinic as I was passing and I have a pair of shoes that need mending."

Perseverance: "It's good to see you. How are you these days Wesley?"

Mr. Wesley: "Pretty good you know, considering......"

Perseverance: "Well, we've put in a good innings."

Mr. Wesley: "Yes, and we're still in there batting."

Perseverance: "Not run out yet."

Mr. Wesley: "Mind you I've had some near misses at the slips."

Perseverance: "Well, we all have to have a few chances to make a good score!"

They are both in their eighties.

Soon after this everyone went their separate ways and Miss Julie closed the Clinic for that week.

"For life, too, is only an instant, only the dissolving of ourselves in the selves of all others as if bestowing a gift........"

Boris Pasternak

Laughing Gulls (photo by Cathy Howie)

Our Laughing Gulls

They will come;
You can be sure of it;
They will be here by April the eighteenth.
You will hear their laughing voices.
First, a few scouts arrive....
I heard their voices faintly
As I swept our room
early in the morning of April the fifteenth;
and then for three days
there was silence again.
But today, April the eighteenth,
We hear the crescendo of our Laughing Gulls
Ha, haaaa, ha, ha, haaaaa
as they arrive en masse
for their time here with us in Antigua.
Their time to nest
and raise their fledglings
teaching them the ways of gulls
before they leave us again
to fly up North
for the winter.

By September the twenty-fifth
they will all be gone;
and suddenly the sky is silent once more.

Welcome, welcome Laughing Gulls
Hello, hello, hellooooe, ha, ha;
I love to hear your voices calling
the truth of nature's continuity
in a world
that changes quickly.

April 18th, 2005

www.ingramcontent.com/pod-product-compliance
Lightning Source LLC
Chambersburg PA
CBHW022032090426

42741CB00007B/1034